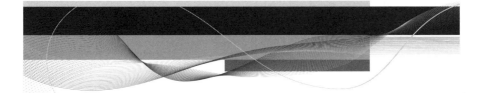

TECHNOLOGY-INFUSED
# French
Foreign-Language Instruction for the Digital Age

Edited by Carl Falsgraf

International Society for Technology in Education
EUGENE, OREGON • WASHINGTON, DC

W9-BXY-634

# Technology-Infused French
## Foreign-Language Instruction for the Digital Age

Edited by Carl Falsgraf

© 2011 International Society for Technology in Education

World rights reserved. No part of this book may be reproduced or transmitted in any form or by any means—electronic, mechanical, photocopying, recording, or by any information storage or retrieval system—without prior written permission from the publisher. Contact Permissions Editor: www.iste.org/permissions/; permissions@iste.org; fax: 1.541.302.3780.

Director of Book Publishing: *Courtney Burkholder*
Acquisitions Editor: *Jeff V. Bolkan*
Production Editors: *Tina Wells, Lynda Gansel*
Production Coordinator: *Rachel Williams*
Graphic Designer: *Signe Landin*
Developmental Editor: *Mike van Mantgem*
Copy Editor: *Anna Drexler*
Proofreader: *Barbara J. Hewick*
Book/Cover Design and Production: *Kim McGovern*

**Library of Congress Cataloging-in-Publication Data**

Technology-infused French: foreign-language instruction for the digital age /
  Carl Falsgraf, Editor.
    p. cm.
  ISBN 978-1-56484-282-4 (pbk.)
  1. French language—Study and teaching—Technological innovations.
  2. French language—Study and teaching.  3. Educational technology.    I. Falsgraf, Carl.
  II. International Society for Technology in Education.
  PC2066.T43 2011
  448.2'40785—dc22

                                                    2010054374

First Edition
ISBN: 978-1-56484-282-4
Printed in the United States of America

Cover image © Ademdemir, Dreamstime.com

ISTE® is a registered trademark of the International Society for Technology in Education.

# About ISTE

The International Society for Technology in Education (ISTE) is the trusted source for professional development, knowledge generation, advocacy, and leadership for innovation. ISTE is the premier membership association for educators and education leaders engaged in improving teaching and learning by advancing the effective use of technology in PK–12 and teacher education.

Home of the National Educational Technology Standards (NETS) and ISTE's annual conference and exposition (formerly known as NECC), ISTE represents more than 100,000 professionals worldwide. We support our members with information, networking opportunities, and guidance as they face the challenge of transforming education. To find out more about these and other ISTE initiatives, visit our website at www.iste.org.

As part of our mission, ISTE Book Publishing works with experienced educators to develop and produce practical resources for classroom teachers, teacher educators, and technology leaders. Every manuscript we select for publication is carefully peer-reviewed and professionally edited. We value your feedback on this book and other ISTE products. E-mail us at books@iste.org.

**International Society for Technology in Education**
Washington, DC, Office:
    1710 Rhode Island Ave. NW, Suite 900, Washington, DC 20036-3132
Eugene, Oregon, Office:
    180 West 8th Ave., Suite 300, Eugene, OR 97401-2916
Order Desk: 1.800.336.5191
Order Fax: 1.541.302.3778
Customer Service: orders@iste.org
Book Publishing: books@iste.org
Book Sales and Marketing: booksmarketing@iste.org
Web: www.iste.org

# About the Editor and Contributors

## Editor

**Carl Falsgraf** is founder and Director of the Center for Applied Second Language Studies (CASLS), a National Foreign Language Resource Center at the University of Oregon. He was president of the Pacific Northwest Council for Languages (PNCFL) and has served on the American Council on the Teaching of Foreign Languages (ACTFL) Executive Council, the Association of Teachers of Japanese (ATJ) Board of Directors, and the Foreign Language Annals (FLA) Editorial Board. He has delivered numerous keynote addresses and workshops, and published papers on second language acquisition, functional linguistics, and standards-based language education. He is the lead designer of the Standards-based Measurement of Proficiency (STAMP) online proficiency assessment and other technology-based tools to help teachers develop and measure student proficiency.

## Contributing Authors, Section 1

Kyle Ennis, vice president, Avant Assessment, Eugene, Oregon (Chapter 2)

Carl Falsgraf, director, CASLS, University of Oregon (Chapter 1)

Rita Oleksak, director, Foreign Languages and Early Language Learning (ELL), Glastonbury Public Schools, Connecticut (Chapter 3)

Kathleen M. Riordan, national consultant, former director of Foreign Languages, Springfield, Massachusetts (Chapter 3)

## Contributing Authors, Section 2

Laurent Cammarata, assistant professor, University of Georgia (Chapter 4)

Marcia Harmon Rosenbusch, director, National K–12 Foreign Language Resource Center, Iowa State University (Chapter 5 Introduction)

Diane J. Tedick, associate professor, University of Minnesota Resource Center (Chapter 4)

**Chapter 4: Unit 1.** Original unit developed by Barbara C. Anderson, French teacher, Edina High School, Edina, Minnesota. Unit adapted by Laurent Cammarata and Diane J. Tedick for this publication.

**Chapter 4: Unit 2.** Original unit developed by Pam Wesely, middle school French teacher, Breck School, Minneapolis, Minnesota, and Ph.D. student, Second Languages and Cultures Education, University of Minnesota. Unit adapted by Laurent Cammarata and Diane J. Tedick for this publication.

**Chapter 5: Unit 3.** Nancy Gadbois, department chair, Foreign Languages, High School of Science and Technology, Springfield, Massachusetts.

**Chapter 5: Unit 4.** Karen Willetts-Kokora, foreign language resource teacher, Springbrook High School, Montgomery County Public Schools, Rockville, Maryland.

# Contents

Contents

## SECTION 2 ▪ Resource Units

### CHAPTER 4

## CoBaLTT Project

### CHAPTER 5

## Iowa State

### APPENDIX A

## Assessment Rubrics for the Resource Units

### APPENDIX B

## Learn More with Additional Resources

### APPENDIX C

## Standards for Foreign Language Learning

# Introduction

## How to Use This Book

This book is divided into two main sections.

### Section 1 • Strategies for Getting Started

Section 1 provides chapters that will help teachers successfully integrate technology into K–12 classrooms. Chapters 1–3 provide teachers with guidelines for integrating technology in foreign language instruction. Teachers also are given ideas on integrating technology standards and foreign language standards, and the role technology plays in performance assessment.

### Section 2 • Resource Units

Section 2 provides teachers with four resource units developed as part of two different projects: the CoBaLTT Project (Content-Based Language Teaching with Technology) and the Iowa State National K–12 Foreign Language Resource Center Project. For each unit, there are three major sections—the Overview, Teaching the Unit, and Unit Assessments.

### Overview

**At a Glance.** At the start of each unit, an overview provides quick at-a-glance information on the unit, including the target age, the ACTFL Proficiency Level, the primary content area, other disciplines that connect through the unit, and the time frame within which the unit can be taught.

**Unit Objectives.** The unit is designed to meet the objectives listed in this section.

**Description.** This is a brief description of the unit, covering topics such as the unit's development and special resources the unit incorporates.

**Standards Addressed.** Standards for Foreign Language Learning (National Standards, 1999, 2006) and National Educational Technology Standards for Students (NETS•S; ISTE, 2007) that are addressed in the unit are listed. Listings of these standards appear in Appendix C and Appendix D and are available online (see page 4).

**Connections to Other Disciplines.** Every unit connects to other disciplines. This section identifies the content that the unit explores as part of the French language lessons.

**Spotlight on Technology.** Each unit highlights the use of one or more types of technology. This section explains how the highlighted technology is incorporated into the lesson plan.

**Technology Resources Needed.** Each unit provides a list of all the hardware and software needed to successfully implement the lesson.

**Supplementary Resources.** This section gives the teacher a list of important websites, books, videos, audio recordings, or other resources that can be used to enhance the lesson. The resources are organized in various ways depending on the unit, to best fit the needs of an educator teaching the unit.

## Teaching the Unit

This section provides a complete teaching plan for the unit, broken into activities and days. Within each section, the subsections "Preview" and "Focused Learning" provide a guide for teachers, and in some activities, the additional subsections "Unit Extension Activities" and "Teaching Tips" offer supplementary instructional ideas.

**Unit Extension Activities and Teaching Tips.** Sometimes lessons are so good, students and teachers don't want them to end. The "Unit Extension Activities" section offers additional unitwide suggestions for extending the lesson for teachers interested in further exploring the topic. Many units offer "Teaching Tips" within each activity, while some units conclude with unitwide "Teaching Tips." These sections help teachers get the most out of the unit as a whole by providing implementation suggestions and insights into which teaching strategy might be the most effective for you.

## Assessing the Units

Assessment ideas are included with each unit. Scoring rubrics appear in Appendix A as well as on the accompanying CD.

**CD: Resources, Unit Supplements.** Tucked in the back cover of *Technology-Infused French* is a CD that contains a wealth of resources, including more detailed unit descriptions, along with handouts (such as worksheets and short stories), and assessment rubrics. The unit material on the CD also includes links to online resources.

## Appendixes

The appendixes provide the assessment rubrics for the resource units (Appendix A), additional relevant resources (Appendix B), the Standards for Foreign Language Learning (Appendix C), and the full National Educational Technology Standards (NETS) for Students and Teachers (Appendix D).

# Beyond This Book

The authors of individual learning activities have designed lessons based on their expertise, but cannot account for the needs of every teaching situation. Therefore, educators should incorporate and modify lessons to fit the circumstances and needs of their students. The sample lessons also provide a lens for reexamining traditional lessons and discovering ways to infuse technology to enrich teaching and learning. Appendix B provides suggestions of resources that will help you learn specific educational technologies in depth.

Be proactive about sharing your good work with others. There are many lesson plan websites as well as school, district, professional association, and parent meetings at which to present new lesson plans and the resulting student work. Educators need to learn from their peers. Educators also need to make parents aware of their efforts to integrate technology and learning in the classroom, and to inform the greater public about how schools are meeting the needs of students, parents, and the community.

# References

International Society for Technology in Education (ISTE). (2007). *National educational technology standards for students.* Eugene, OR: Author.

National Standards in Foreign Language Education Project. (1999, 2006). *Standards for foreign language learning in the 21st century* (3rd ed.). Alexandria, VA: American Council on the Teaching of Foreign Languages (ACTFL).

## Online Resources

International Society for Technology in Education (ISTE), Eugene, Oregon
www.iste.org

*National Educational Technology Standards*
www.iste.org/nets

American Council on the Teaching of Foreign Languages (ACTFL), Alexandria, Virginia
www.actfl.org

*National Standards for Foreign Language Education*
www.actfl.org/i4a/pages/index.cfm?pageid=3392

# SECTION 1

# Strategies for Getting Started

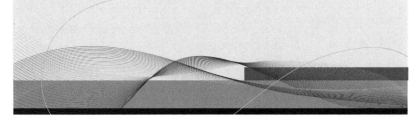

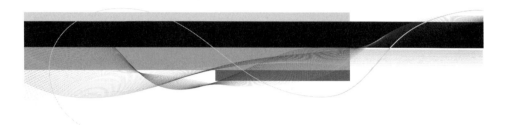

### CHAPTER 1

# Learner-Friendly Technology in a Brain-Friendly Classroom

## Appropriate Technology in the Service of Proficiency

*Carl Falsgraf*

In this chapter we will explore our mission as foreign language teachers and how technology can help us fulfill that mission.

## Meaningful Content in Realistic Contexts

We all understand that our mission is proficiency: every student able to communicate meaningful content in realistic contexts. How can we create realistic contexts in our classrooms? Role-plays are great and pair work is wonderful, but at some level, students know that this is playacting. The content of what they are talking about, the cultural context in which they are operating, is contrived. They are not communicating with a community of real people, but a contrived community of personas. The best—the most appropriate—use of technology in the second language classroom is to provide authentic, contextualized interactive tasks with members of the target language community. Let's break that down.

## Authentic

The definition of an authentic text is one that is written by native speakers for native speakers. Authentic oral communication can either be speech between native speakers or speech to or from a nonnative speaker *for a real-life purpose*. Think about what a student hears from you on a typical day. First, how much of that speech is in English? Clearly, not authentic. Using English to teach the target language alters the authenticity of the learning environment. Second, how much is for pedagogic purpose? Also, out the door. Though using the target language for instruction is necessary, focusing solely on this purpose alters the authenticity of the learning environment. Now, how much of the target language does the student hear that is for a real-life purpose? Perhaps greetings, some housekeeping matters, an occasional exchange in the hall. How can we expect students to succeed in authentic contexts when they never experience one? Technology can help.

## Contextualized

Authentic language always appears in an authentic context. Pedagogic language rarely does. We read the paper for information. We read labels to make sure foods don't have anything we are allergic to. Context aids our understanding because we expect to find certain information in certain places. For instance, you never see stock quotes or poems on the side of a macaroni and cheese box. Context helps us focus on our specific task. The expectations established by a specific context help focus language-learners in the classroom. We have all encountered unfocused, off-task students in our classrooms. Maybe it is because we just gave them a reading passage called "José's Diary," in which he tells us how he gets ready for school in the morning. Though this may be useful for contrasting the preterit and imperfect, it serves no real-life purpose and has no authentic context. Textbooks are, strictly speaking, a context, but not one that will do you much good in the real world. This is what people mean when they say, "I studied two years of French, but when I went to Paris I couldn't say a thing." Of course not. Granted, they had never been to France, but also they had never experienced speaking French in an authentic context. So, how do we incorporate an authentic context in foreign language instruction? Technology can help.

## Interactive

How often do students get a chance to interact with authentic, contextualized texts—spoken or written—in our classrooms? Not often enough. The major focus of second language acquisition studies over the past 15 years or so has been on the effect of interaction. In study after study, students have demonstrated that they learn better when interacting with others. Play a recording of a native speaker describing how to put together a puzzle and about 40% of the new vocabulary contained in the instructions is retained. Have a real person there to describe the same thing and more than 60% is retained. Why? Two reasons:

1. As human beings, we are wired to remember more emotionally intense events. A monkey watches the rain fall and forgets it. A monkey gets chased by a lion and never forgets it. Interactions among human beings involve complex emotions that become associated with words, helping us to remember them.

2. Two-way communication allows for back channels (responses such as "Huh?" and "What's that?") and other devices to increase the comprehensibility of a passage. How much interaction happens in the typical language classroom? Not enough. How can we resolve this? Technology can help.

## Tasks

A task is an activity with a concrete, nonlinguistic, realistic goal that requires language to reach that goal. Notice that the goal is not linguistic, but that it requires language to accomplish that goal. In other words, it is authentic. In real life, how often do we say, "I think I need to brush up on my conjugations: *go, went, gone; come, came, come; amo, amas, amat*"? However, we have plenty of authentic tasks in our lives that require language. You want your kids to do their homework (use imperatives!); you want your principal to give you a bigger classroom next year (use modals and interrogatives!); you want to tell a joke (use narrative past!).

The beauty of tasks is that just as we focus on a goal and let the language take care of itself, students engaged in tasks also are focused on the content of what they are doing, not the forms they must use. Consequently, tasks are extremely valuable as a means for building fluency and for making language automatic. A few years ago, I started doing oral assessment in Oregon with colleagues at the Center for Applied Second Language Studies (CASLS) and Language Learning Solutions (now Avant Assessment). Initially, teachers complained bitterly when students who "knew" the topics of weather or family or food did not pass the oral performance assessment. We showed these teachers the videos of their students being asked "So what did you eat for breakfast?" and their students sitting there tongue-tied. The teachers' most common reaction was, "But we covered food in Chapter 3!" Yes, it was covered. Yes, the student "had" words to describe food. But the response was not automatic because the vocabulary was not acquired; it was just memorized. Unlike rote memorization, tasks allow us to take language knowledge and develop it into language proficiency. So why in the world would we do anything else when we use technology to teach language?

So, to review, our technology checklist looks something like this:

- Is it authentic?

- Is it contextualized?

- Is it interactive?

- Is it task-oriented?

# More on Proficiency

The proficiency movement began in the 1980s with the publication of the ACTFL Proficiency Guidelines. Its vision was revolutionary: the purpose of language teaching is to prepare students to communicate meaningful content in realistic situations. While *proficiency* is the buzzword that everybody uses, in most classrooms the majority of time is still spent developing formal knowledge through explanations, drills, or worksheets. The same is true of standards: everybody thinks they are great, but standards-based classrooms are few and far between.

Why is there such a gap between what we say and what we do? Although most teachers want to focus on proficiency standards, most lack the time and expertise to develop materials, lesson plans, and assessments, and therefore they continue to follow a textbook. But it isn't entirely fair to blame teachers. With growing class sizes, few teachers have the time to create special lessons, materials, and tests.

Technology can help us become efficient enough to individualize instruction, to plan for proficiency, to measure students' progress toward the goal of communicating effectively in realistic situations. This is not a pipe dream; the tools are available today. Many of them are described in this volume. Anybody who can order a book online can use these tools to improve their teaching. There is nothing to be afraid of here. We have not created a monster. Technology in our classrooms is no more likely to take over our lives than vacuum cleaners are. If we remain focused on the goal of proficiency—using these tools to improve student performance—we will surely prevail in our struggle.

# Technology's Role in Education

Technology can be scary. We have a love/hate relationship with technology accompanied with paradoxical expectations: the hope that it will solve all our problems and the fear that it will take over our lives. Neither is a real possibility, but it sometimes seems so when we see a whiz-bang demonstration of the latest gizmo or, conversely, when we feel the abject panic that arises the moment following a computer lab crash as we're facing a class of thirty 14-year-olds with nothing to distract them from following their basest impulses.

Most language teachers come to the field with training in literature and language, not technology. It makes sense, therefore, to look to literature to tell us about our attitudes toward technology, to review our understanding of how students learn, and from there to explore ways that technology can help us make our classrooms more compatible with our educational goals.

## Literature and Technology

As Kyle Ennis points out in Chapter 2, the most critical factor in ensuring effective use of technology in the classroom is the teacher's attitude about technology. If the teacher appears skeptical of the virtues of technology, the students will be as well. This distrust of technology has a history. Early science-fiction pioneers Mary Shelley and Jules Verne imagined the implications of technology on society, revealing our paradoxical love/hate relationship with man-made machines. Before then, thinkers and writers had envisioned utopian societies, such as Jefferson's nation of small, independent farmers, or apocalyptic religious visions, such as Dante's inferno, but Shelley and Verne added the notion of technology as the source of that utopia or that hell. Let's start with hell and work upward.

If you have seen Frankenstein movies, you know that Dr. Frankenstein "created a monster" by playing God and using two cutting-edge technologies of the time—surgery and electricity. His creation then escaped, taking on a life of its own and terrorizing the population. The Frankenstein metaphor has come to symbolize the dangers of scientific hubris and our fear of technological inventions that we scarcely understand. This metaphor has become more powerful as the technology that terrifies us has gone from electricity and surgery in Shelley's time (the 1800s), to gas chambers and atom bombs in the time of the early Frankenstein films (the 1900s), to the computer databases of today that seem to document our every move, including which genetically modified foods we bought for last night's dinner. Technology has always been scary.

But Shelley's original monster was quite different from Hollywood actor Boris Karloff's interpretation, which likens the monster to a grizzly bear—wild roaring, arms stiff and reaching to dismember the innocent—as though Dr. Frankenstein implanted the brain of a grizzly bear in the monster, as though the monster was not human. Shelley's monster, however, had a normal human brain. In fact there are long passages revealing the monster's philosophical musings on the notion of identity, the relationship between the individual and society, and the nature of prejudice. The monster is misunderstood and persecuted because of his appearance and the nature of his birth.

Shelley's *Frankenstein* is not just about the terrifying implications of technology—the creation of an uncontrollable monster—but about us and our irrational fears of the unknown, the new, and the different. Shelley's genius is that she captured both the means of destruction— runaway technology—and the social conditions that enable such horrors to be unleashed—hatred, intolerance, and mob psychology.

Are you a villager, torch in hand, convinced that the monster is a menace on the loose? Or are you the young girl who was able to see past her fear, understand the heart of the monster, and befriend it?

Jules Verne had a different vision of the implications of technology. He envisioned technology strengthening the human spirit by generating imaginative and incredible experiences. As Phileas Fogg, Verne's protagonist, resolves to circumnavigate the world, we see that our curiosity in the nature of the world may lead us to unprecedented knowledge and prosperity. Like Shelley, Verne was prescient. Technology, whether it be hot-air balloons, automobiles, or spacecraft, can provide us with experiences that expand the mind and feed the spirit.

Jules Verne had the spirit of a teacher. He believed that the human condition could be improved through the expansion of knowledge. He was optimistic about the future—as all teachers need to be. Jules Verne was what would now be called an early adopter: the kind of guy who rushes out to get the latest model of computer or smartphone and can't wait to upgrade his operating system and download the latest apps.

Are you an early adopter, a latter-day Phileas Fogg willing to get in the balloon and trust that you will come down somewhere safe?

We should be neither villagers giving in to our Philistine instincts of destroying what is new and unfamiliar nor Vernian heroes setting off in untested contraptions. The model for a healthy approach to technology is—and it pains me deeply to say this—

Star Wars. While he pales in comparison as a literary figure, George Lucas got it right on our modern relationship with technology.

The *Star Wars* series is best known for its special effects. The audience may be thrilled, but the characters don't even bat an eye. The *Star Wars* heroes are neither fearful nor enamored of the technology at their disposal. Luke Skywalker and his sidekicks prevail against superior technology—such as the Death Star—with their relatively rudimentary spacecraft and weapons. The key to their success—and ours—is a superior sense of spiritual purpose. It is the Force, not the fancy gizmos, that ensures ultimate victory. Parlor tricks such as levitating objects are merely exercises to cultivate spiritual discipline and strength, not ends in and of themselves. The good guys are as likely to take down an enemy with a club as with a laser gun. Light sabers are cool, but really, they are just high-tech swords. But they do the trick. Just like chalkboards.

## Conclusion: Language Teaching and Technology

So let's assume we are neither villagers in the mob bent on killing the monster nor Phileas Fogg willing to try any newfangled gizmo that comes along. We are Luke Skywalkers: We are willing and able to use whatever low-tech or high-tech tools are at our disposal to accomplish our mission. May the Force be with you!

## Reference

American Council on the Teaching of Foreign Languages (ACTLF). (1986). *ACTFL proficiency guidelines*. Yonkers, NY: Author.

CHAPTER **2**

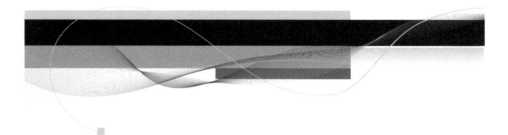

# The NETS·S and the Five Cs

Integrating Technology and Foreign Language Standards

*Kyle Ennis*

This chapter will introduce the Standards for Foreign Language Learning and discuss ways that technology can enhance and focus these broad areas of study. We will also look at the NETS·S through the lens of the foreign language classroom and explore areas of possible connection.

New state and national K–12 education standards have been established over the last several years that delineate high expectations for students and teachers. The result is a heightened awareness of accountability in the classroom. While most educators view this as a good development, many also feel somewhat overwhelmed by all they must know and do to help their students meet these standards. This chapter strives to bring some clarity to this complicated state of affairs by offering a quick summary of both the foreign language content area standards adopted (and co-developed) by the American Council on the Teaching of Foreign Languages (ACTFL; National Standards in Foreign Language Education Project, 1999, 2006) and ISTE's National Educational Technology Standards for Students (NETS•S; 2007), and suggesting ways that foreign language teachers can effectively address both sets of standards in the classroom.

Because the foreign language field is not generally considered to be a core content area, it has not received as much public or political attention as math, science, or language arts. Nevertheless, foreign language standards have been in use for several years—well ahead of standards in these core content areas. In 1993, the ACTFL coordinated a national effort to develop and publish foreign language standards as a collaborative activity with various language-specific organizations: the American Association of Teachers of French (AATF), the American Association of Teachers of German (AATG), the American Association of Teachers of Spanish and Portuguese (AATSP), the National Council of Secondary Teachers of Japanese (NCSTJ, since renamed the National Council of Japanese Language Teachers, NCJLT), and others. These standards were adopted in 1996, updated in 1999 and then again in 2006 to include Arabic (National Standards, 1999, 2006). The five categories of standards that were developed—Communication, Cultures, Connections, Comparisons, and Communities, now known fondly as the "Five Cs"—outline critical areas of student focus in foreign language learning (Figure 2.1).

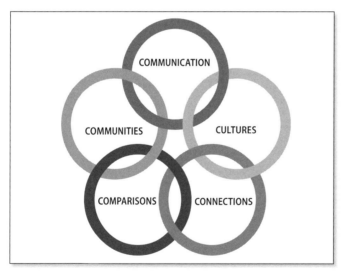

**Figure 2.1.** The Five Cs of the Standards for Foreign Language Learning.
*Reprinted with permission of the American Council on the Teaching of Foreign Languages.*

K–12 Performance Guidelines were also developed to describe the specific levels of proficiency through which students should progress as they acquire a foreign language. Individual states have subsequently elaborated on these national standards to develop detailed state-level guidelines that clearly articulate expected learner outcomes connected to the Five Cs and the K–12 Performance Guidelines.

As we review the Standards for Foreign Language Learning, some may ask: Why five Cs, and not six? Why not add computers to this model? Shouldn't technology be included in these standards for foreign language learning? These are appropriate questions as they indicate the need for more information on technology integration in the foreign language classroom. This book aims to fill that need.

This chapter outlines an integration process that you can easily utilize in your classroom. However, to better understand the attitudes that may surround this issue, it is important that we first tackle the notion that foreign language teachers should concern themselves only with teaching their specialized content and that someone else should instruct students on the use of technology or computers. Nothing could be further from the truth. If our goal is to help students gain ever higher levels of language proficiency, we need to familiarize ourselves and become comfortable using every available teaching tool and resource that will move our students closer to language proficiency. Today, this means learning how to integrate technology in our teaching practices.

The ISTE NETS•S identify what students should know and be able to do with technology to accomplish tasks and enhance their learning across the curriculum. The underlying assumption of this book is that foreign language teachers should become familiar with these standards and actively seek to integrate technology in meaningful ways to assist student learning. This does not mean that we think foreign language content should take a back seat or be considered less important than the technology that delivers that content. Instead, we simply want to help teachers weave technology seamlessly and effectively into their curriculum, so they can support student achievement in both the foreign language and the technology standards.

The final section of this chapter presents a series of charts that links these two sets of standards (the Standards for Foreign Language Learning and NETS•S) and outlines activities and ideas that can support and improve the teaching and learning of foreign languages. It is important to emphasize at the outset, however, that technology standards should not be considered extra baggage that will slow and hinder progress in achieving the Five Cs. Instead, when integrated effectively, technology can make our classrooms more instructive and meaningful places that will foster higher levels of student involvement and language proficiency.

# Standards for Foreign Language Learning

In introducing the Standards for Foreign Language Learning, we will look briefly at the language created by the ACTFL and the coalition groups responsible for creating the standards. These standards outline critical focal points for which students should develop skills as they acquire languages. Work on the standards began in 1993 through a grant dedicated for this purpose, with representative groups from each of the national language associations—AATF, AATG, AATSP, NCSTJ, and others. Representatives from each of these organizations worked to draft the global areas of the standards and define the scope of each broad goal. They also worked closely with other educational organizations as well as business and community leaders to ensure broad acceptance of the standards.

Once these standards were drafted and approved, other task forces were charged with the mission of creating content requirements and key learning scenarios that more fully detailed the standards in action. Now known as the Five Cs, these standard categories outline key instruction that all students in foreign language education should encounter as part of their learning. The Five Cs are identified as: Communication, Cultures, Connections, Comparisons, and Communities.

- **Communication** is at the heart of the standards, underscoring the notion that communication with others is the central goal in learning a foreign language.

- **Cultures** stresses that through study of other languages, students gain a knowledge and understanding of the cultures that use the language. Students can't really master the language until they have mastered the cultural contexts in which the language occurs.

- **Connections** is the idea that learning another language will give students an opportunity to connect with other content areas through the lens of the language they are studying, allowing them to learn new concepts in new ways.

- **Comparisons** focuses upon the idea that learning a foreign language will allow students an opportunity to compare and contrast their immediate world to that of the language they are learning, giving them broader appreciation for their own language and culture, while also helping them to acquire appreciation and acceptance of other languages and cultures.

- **Communities** focuses on the need to reach outside the classroom to interact with others in meaningful ways, using the target language. This challenging standard calls for students and teachers to think creatively about how the language can be used to accomplish real-world tasks and how they can endeavor to use the language in their communities. Focusing on this goal helps teachers motivate students to use the language they are learning, to see applications of the concepts in real-world situations, and to understand that language learning is a lifelong process.

The Five Cs establish a framework foundation that outlines the areas of instruction that students should encounter as they progress through language programs. Although the standards do not detail the specifics of what students should be able to do or describe how well they should be able to accomplish those tasks, they serve as guiding principles for language educators and administrators in terms of the broad topics that should be addressed. Each standard can be further defined with progress indicators for Grades 4, 8, and 12. (The ACTFL provides sample progress indicators at its website, www.actfl.org > Publications > Standards for Foreign Language Learning: Executive Summary (PDF).) Again, although technology is not specifically included in these standards, it is easy to see areas where technology could be used to support their achievement.

## Standards for Foreign Language Learning

### Communication

Communicate in Languages Other Than English

- **Standard 1.1.** Students engage in conversations, provide and obtain information, express feelings and emotions, and exchange opinions.

- **Standard 1.2.** Students understand and interpret written and spoken language on a variety of topics.

- **Standard 1.3.** Students present information, concepts, and ideas to an audience of listeners or readers on a variety of topics.

### Cultures

Gain Knowledge and Understanding of Other Cultures

- **Standard 2.1.** Students demonstrate an understanding of the relationship between the practices and perspectives of the culture studied.

- **Standard 2.2.** Students demonstrate an understanding of the relationship between the products and perspectives of the culture studied.

### Connections

Connect with Other Disciplines and Acquire Information

- **Standard 3.1.** Students reinforce and further their knowledge of other disciplines through the foreign language.

- **Standard 3.2.** Students acquire information and recognize the distinctive viewpoints that are only available through the foreign language and its culture.

### Comparisons

Develop Insight into the Nature of Language and Culture

- **Standard 4.1.** Students demonstrate understanding of the nature of language through comparisons of the language studied and their own.

- **Standard 4.2.** Students demonstrate understanding of the concept of culture through comparisons of the cultures studied and their own.

### Communities

Participate in Multilingual Communities at Home and Around the World

- **Standard 5.1.** Students use the language both within and beyond the school setting.

- **Standard 5.2.** Students show evidence of becoming lifelong learners by using the language for personal enjoyment and enrichment.

*To learn more about the Five Cs and the Standards for Foreign Language Learning, visit the ACTFL website at www.actfl.org. Reprinted with permission from the National Standards in Foreign Language Education Project.*

# Performance Guidelines

Beyond these general content standards, the ACTFL has defined proficiency levels for how well students should be able to communicate in the language they are learning, from Novice through Pre-Advanced levels. These levels are described in the K–12 Performance Guidelines and further incorporated into state- and district-level documents.

Technology integration, however, is not fully addressed in these standards. We need to look to the NETS•S to help determine what students should be able to do with technology as they study the language and to define how we as teachers can use technology both to enhance learning and to help students acquire skills that will support them as lifelong learners of the language.

To better understand these technology standards, we will examine the NETS•S and their parameters for student learning. As you review these technology standards, consider ways that each could be addressed as part of your current classroom activities. Reflect also upon your current use of technology and seek ways to enhance instruction through the inclusion of these standards within your instruction.

# National Educational Technology Standards for Students

The National Educational Technology Standards for Students (NETS•S ) identify the skills and knowledge that students require to learn effectively and live productively in an increasingly digital society. The six categories are broad enough to be easily applied across all content areas, yet detailed enough to communicate clear expectations of technology use and integration. Teachers should use the standards as they plan for activities, looking for natural areas of integration that support the standards while at the same time applying technology in a manner that better facilitates teaching and learning. The full text for the standards appears in Appendix D and can be viewed online at www.iste.org/nets/.

Similar to the Five Cs, these standards suggest general areas of student focus. On close investigation of these standards, one learns quickly that they have been written to support learning and education in a very broad sense. No single class or course could incorporate all of these standards. It must be a coordinated collaborative effort across the curriculum if these standards are to be achieved.

As foreign language teachers, we have a shared responsibility to address these standards and seek opportunities to include elements of technology in our lessons that expose our students to the power and purpose of technology in language learning and support our instructional goals. The key to this integration is a clear understanding of the technologies that are available to assist in achieving these standards.

# Bringing the Next "C" into Focus

In this section, we will look at how the foreign language standards and NETS•S can be combined to support both the learning of a language and the acquisition of technology skills. We will approach this from the perspective of a foreign language teacher and will include integration strategies that showcase how technology could be used to support both the foreign language standards as well as the NETS•S. The list of ideas is not exhaustive. More than anything else, these ideas should act as a catalyst to expand attitudes about how technology could be used to support teaching and learning in the foreign language classroom.

## COMMUNICATION

| Standards for Foreign Language Learning | Technology-Based Activities and NETS•S |
|---|---|
| **Communicate in Languages Other Than English**<br><br>**Standard 1.1.** Students engage in conversations, provide and obtain information, express feelings and emotions, and exchange opinions.<br><br>**Standard 1.2.** Students understand and interpret written and spoken language on a variety of topics.<br><br>**Standard 1.3.** Students present information, concepts, and ideas to an audience of listeners or readers on a variety of topics. | ▪ Teachers can incorporate online resources that allow students to record their voices on a computer, MP3 recording device, or cell phone and immediately listen to their recording. Teachers can use this technology to collect speaking samples without the need for tapes and recorders or dedicated language labs. **NETS•S 2.a, c, d; 3.b, c, d; 4.a, b; 6.a, b**<br><br>▪ Teachers can utilize online resources to evaluate student reading, writing, listening, and speaking skills to track progress and identify proficiency levels. The use of technology in this area will allow teachers to collect large amounts of student achievement and proficiency data in an efficient, effective, and powerful way. **NETS•S 2.a, c, d; 3.b, c, d; 4.a, b, d; 6.a, b**<br><br>▪ Teachers can institute e-mail pals/instant messaging relationships with other classes. Students can exchange e-mails and messages with students from around the world in the target language. This activity is a new play on the pen-pals concept with immediate results, rather than lengthy waiting periods between exchanges. This is a great way to teach keyboarding skills in the target language (i.e., the proper use of accented characters and character sets for languages such as Japanese, Chinese, Korean, and Arabic). **NETS•S 2.a, c, d; 3.b, c, d; 4.a, b; 6.a, b**<br><br>▪ Students can complete WebQuests that expose them to web pages from the target language/culture. They will experience realia in the form of web pages, with guided direction from the teacher or WebQuest creator. **NETS•S 2.a, b, c, d; 3.a, b, c, d; 4.a, b, d; 5.a, b**<br><br>▪ Students can research topics connected with learning a foreign language and present them to a class of peers using electronic presentation forms, web pages, or print publications, including photo, video, and audio elements that better showcase the research topic and enhance the presentation. **NETS•S 1.a, b; 2.a, b, c, d; 3.a, b, c, d; 4.a, b, d; 5.a, b**<br><br>▪ Teachers can employ the use of video recording equipment and computer editing software to collect speech and presentation samples from students and showcase these to other classes or archive them in electronic portfolio collections that catalog student proficiencies. **NETS•S 2.a, b, c, d; 3.a, b, c, d; 4.a, b, d; 5.a, b** |

## CULTURES

| Standards for Foreign Language Learning | Technology-Based Activities and NETS·S |
|---|---|
| **Gain Knowledge and Understanding of Other Cultures**<br><br>**Standard 2.1.** Students demonstrate an understanding of the relationship between the practices and perspectives of the culture studied.<br><br>**Standard 2.2.** Students demonstrate an understanding of the relationship between the products and perspectives of the culture studied. | ■ Teachers can assign students to research elements of the target culture and then build electronic presentations or websites that share what they learned with the class. **NETS·S 1.a, b, c, d; 2.a, b, c, d; 3.a, b, c, d; 4.a, b, d; 5.a, b**<br><br>■ Students can create online or print surveys that can be delivered to both same-language and target language individuals and then tabulate results and share findings with their class. This builds a greater understanding of the key cultural components of the target culture. **NETS·S 1.a; 2.a, b, c, d; 3.a, b, c, d; 4.a, b, d; 5.a, b; 6.a, b**<br><br>■ Teachers can construct a web activity in which students engage in a structured search of the web for sites that showcase cultural icons or products of the target language/culture. Students can then share their findings in electronic presentations to the class. **NETS·S 1.a; 2.a, b, c, d; 3.a, b, c, d; 4.a, b, d; 5.a, b; 6.a, b** |

## CONNECTIONS

| Standards for Foreign Language Learning | Technology-Based Activities and NETS·S |
|---|---|
| **Connect with Other Disciplines and Acquire Information**<br><br>**Standard 3.1.** Students reinforce and further their knowledge of other disciplines through the foreign language.<br><br>**Standard 3.2.** Students acquire information and recognize the distinctive viewpoints that are only available through the foreign language and its cultures. | ■ Students can utilize online resources to access content for other disciplines in the target language/culture. This can be done by locating educational support sites for these content areas, developed for speakers of the target language. **NETS·S 1.a; 2.a, b, c, d; 3.a, b, c, d; 4.a, b, d; 5.a, b; 6.a, b**<br><br>■ Teachers can direct student projects in which students research a content area of their choice by utilizing a variety of electronic resources and then present their projects in the form of mini lessons or digital stories to the entire class. **NETS·S 1.a; 2.a, b, c, d; 3.a, b, c, d; 4.a, b, d; 5.a, b; 6.a, b** |

**NOTE:** *This particular standard, **Connections**, is a great challenge in any instructional setting. It requires a high degree of language proficiency for both students and teachers, as well as outside experience and access to other content area support. Though challenging, it should not be neglected. Technology will assist in this area in many ways, allowing access to critical content information needed to make these connections possible for the students.*

## COMPARISONS

| Standards for Foreign Language Learning | Technology-Based Activities and NETS·S |
|---|---|
| **Develop Insight into the Nature of Language and Culture**<br><br>**Standard 4.1.** Students demonstrate understanding of the nature of language through comparisons of the language studied and their own.<br><br>**Standard 4.2.** Students demonstrate understanding of the concept of culture through comparisons of the cultures studied and their own. | ■ Through the use of video and audio resources, teachers can showcase sociolinguistic elements of the target language/culture. Students can also access a variety of online resources that utilize video and audio elements as components of their delivery system. Many news and information sites on the Internet now include short video elements that can be viewed on a regular basis. This allows an almost endless resource of real-world language, which can be used in a variety of ways. **NETS·S 1.a; 2.a, b, c, d; 3.a, b, c, d; 4.a, b, d; 5.a, b; 6.a, b**<br><br>■ Teachers can direct student projects in which students research a specific social or cultural issue. Students can create survey or interview sessions that will allow them to gather information from individuals and then transfer the information to spreadsheets. This will allow comparisons and contrasts of the viewpoints of those surveyed or interviewed. **NETS·S 1.a; 2.a, b, c, d; 3.a, b, c, d; 4.a, b, d; 5.a, b; 6.a, b** |

## COMMUNITIES

| Standards for Foreign Language Learning | Technology-Based Activities and NETS·S |
|---|---|
| **Participate in Multilingual Communities at Home and Around the World**<br><br>**Standard 5.1.** Students use the language both within and beyond the school setting.<br><br>**Standard 5.2.** Students show evidence of becoming lifelong learners by using the language for personal enjoyment and enrichment. | ■ Videoconferencing allows teachers to connect with classrooms around the world and with individuals outside the traditional school classroom. Skype and other videoconferencing tools, used in connection with a computer's built-in video or smartphone cameras and CUSeeMe technologies, have made it easy to communicate in ways only imagined just a few short years ago. **NETS·S 1.a; 2.a, b, c, d; 3.a, b, c, d; 4.a, b, d; 5.a, b; 6.a, b**<br><br>■ Students now have access to both online and CD resources that allow them to continue their studies and learning outside the classroom. Many high quality language learning resources are available to assist students in the continuation of studying and learning beyond the classroom. These tools, more dynamic than traditional print-based text systems, include video segments, audio files, and detailed images to assist in the learning process and let the students move at their own pace. Technology has made lifelong learning much easier to accomplish, because of the ease of access that we now enjoy. **NETS·S 1.a; 2.a, b, c, d; 3.a, b, c, d; 4.a, b, d; 5.a, b, c; 6.a, b** |

# Conclusion

While standards are powerful tools to direct student learning, the attitudes that we hold in regard to the standards are ultimately most critical. If we, as educators, see the value in the standards, integrate them into our daily education plans, and communicate them to all of the stakeholders—administrators, students, and parents—we will succeed in incorporating them in a way that makes sense for all participants in the learning process. The challenge is that standards are almost always externally created or dictated and easy integration is not the norm. Standards often mean change, and any amount of change takes time, effort, and dedication. As we consider the integration of technology standards, the process is further complicated by the level of comfort we ourselves have with using technology. Research has clearly shown that the best way to teach technology skills is through applying appropriate technology resources to accomplish tasks and solve problems. By modeling the use of technology in our lessons and activities, we can demonstrate the innumerable advantages of using technology to advance foreign language fluency, and our students will learn very quickly the value of learning with technology.

No other discipline has shown a need for technology more than foreign languages. A variety of skills must be acquired in the foreign language classroom, each requiring continual practice with reading, writing, speaking, and listening, and there is no easy way to accomplish this daunting learning task without the use of technology. At the heart of the technology standards is the notion that technology education is not about "learning how to use computers," but rather the conviction that we can use technology in educational settings in a way that supports teachers in meeting their goals and ultimately assists students in accomplishing meaningful tasks. The challenge for true integration of technology continues to be based on how we view our classroom. If we view our language classrooms as sealed containers where the teacher and textbook are all that are needed to teach, instruct, and lead the students, technology will be considered a hindrance to the goal of language acquisition and will be ignored. If, however, we view our classrooms as portals to the world and the languages we teach, we will discover that technology allows our students to break out of the physical constraints of the textbook and the classroom, enabling them to communicate with others, connect with different disciplines, compare and contrast unfamiliar cultures with their own, and reach into their world communities in meaningful and exciting ways.

# References

International Society for Technology in Education (ISTE). (2007). *National educational technology standards for students.* Eugene, OR: Author.

National Standards in Foreign Language Education Project. (1999, 2006). *Standards for foreign language learning in the 21st century* (3rd ed.). Alexandria, VA: American Council on the Teaching of Foreign Languages (ACTFL).

National Standards in Foreign Language Education Project. (n.d.). *Standards for foreign language education.* Retrieved from www.actfl.org/i4a/pages/index.cfm?pageid=3392

## CHAPTER 3

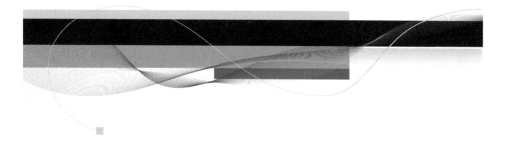

# Measuring What Matters
## Performance Assessment and Technology

*Rita Oleksak and Kathleen M. Riordan*

In this chapter, we will discuss the use of technology to improve both our instruction and our assessment, and, as a result, to provide our students with the opportunity to become proficient in another language so that they may become full citizens of the United States and of the global society. Using a positive and reflective approach, we will consider the importance of performance assessment, the use of technology to help educators organize and contextualize good performance assessments, and the relationship between performance assessment and online tests.

The International Year of Languages in 2008 was a campaign to promote the idea that people who can communicate in at least two languages are a great asset to the communities in which they live and work (Pufahl, Rhodes, & Christian, 2004/2005). The Department of Defense recently convened a national language conference to discuss how to make the United States a language-competent nation. Since the publication of Standards for Foreign Language Learning, classroom teachers have expanded the scope of language teaching to include culture, connections to other disciplines, comparisons among languages and cultures, and participation in multi-lingual communities.

All of these are indicative of a sea change in the foreign language field. Language study used to be a credential of the properly educated, earned through disciplined memorization of vocabulary and grammar rules. Now, language learning develops the ability to truly communicate not just through linguistic mastery, but through a deeper understanding of how, when, and why to say what to whom (National Standards in Foreign Language Education Project, 1999, 2006; n.d.). The success of this enterprise has profound implications for society, the economy, and the national defense. With the purpose of language education changing so significantly, it follows that the way we assess students must also change. Measuring student ability to conjugate verbs or memorize lists of words is no longer sufficient if we are to educate a generation of students to participate in the global economy and society.

---

### 2008: International Year of Languages

On 16 May 2007 the United Nations General Assembly proclaimed 2008 the International Year of Languages. In this context the General Assembly invited Member States, the United Nations system, and all other relevant stakeholders to develop, support, and intensify activities aimed at fostering respect for and the promotion and protection of all languages, in particular endangered languages, linguistic diversity, and multilingualism.

---

## The Base of Assessment

The resource *ACTFL Proficiency Guidelines* (ACTFL, 1986, 2000) has influenced our profession for more than 25 years, first, in the area of assessment, and second, in the area of curriculum development. These guidelines describe language proficiency regardless of where and how it is acquired.

In 1993, foreign language education became the seventh subject area to receive federal funding to develop national K–12 standards. The task force faced the huge task of defining content standards—what students should know and be able to do.

Three major organizing principles were used in developing the standards for foreign language learning.

The first includes the broad goals of language instruction, also known as the Five Cs—Communication, Cultures, Connections, Comparisons, and Communities. (See Chapter 2 for more on the Five Cs.) The second involves the curricular elements necessary for the attainment of the standards, which include a language system, cultural knowledge, communication strategies, critical thinking skills, learning strategies, other subject areas, and technology. The third encompasses the framework of the communicative approach to language teaching, which places primary emphasis on the context and purpose of communication (Brecht & Walton, 1994). The three communicative modes are Interpersonal, Interpretive, and Presentational.

The publication *ACTFL Performance Guidelines for K–12 Learners* (ACTFL, 1998) expands on the previously mentioned guidelines by focusing on language use by students who participate in all levels of foreign language learning. Just as the Standards for Foreign Language Learning are content standards that define the *what* of foreign language learning, the performance guidelines are standards that define *how well*. The guidelines place a student's performance on a proficiency continuum.

## Performance Assessment Fundamentals

Four basic principles should guide teachers in developing quality assessments:

1. Test what is taught.

2. Test the material in the way it was taught.

3. Focus on what students can do.

4. Capture creative language by learners.

Following these criteria, performance-based assessment is authentic and realistic, and it incorporates real-world tasks. Performance assessment calls for the student to construct a response within a context (Lewin & Shoemaker, 1998). Performance assessments have two parts: a clearly defined task—called a product descriptor—and a list of explicit criteria for assessing students' performance or product—called a rubric (Blaz, 2001, p. 17). A performance-based format requires learners to demonstrate their level of competence and knowledge by creating a product as a response (Koda, 1998), hence the presentational piece.

## ACTFL Performance Guidelines for K–12 Learners for Foreign Language Learning

### Novice Low

- Uses isolated words and a few high-frequency phrases to talk about very specific subjects, such as numbers, colors, and the names of common objects.

### Novice Mid

- Uses isolated words, memorized phrases, and occasional formulaic or stock phrases to talk about certain specific learned topics, such as weather, food, and names of family members.
- May contain long hesitations, silences, and/or repetitions and/or reversion to L1.
- May have poor pronunciation.

### Novice High

- Shows emerging ability to create with language by expanding on learned material.
- Relies on personalized recombinations of words, phrases, and stock phrases.
- Shows sporadic and inconsistent creation of sentences.
- Uses simple vocabulary to talk about personal and limited topics.
- May have long hesitations and/or repetitions and/or reversion to L1.
- May appear surprisingly fluent and accurate due to reliance on memorized utterances.

### Intermediate Low

- Shows ability to create with the language using basic novel sentences marked by frequent errors of word choice and verb formation.
- Uses limited, simple, basic vocabulary to talk about topics related to self, family, friends, and everyday life.
- Produces little variety of information.
- Shows emerging control of the present tense and near future.
- Response may be halting with frequent groping for words and occasional reversion to L1.
- May have poor pronunciation.

### Intermediate Mid

- Shows ability to create with the language using a variety of disconnected, discrete sentences with some errors in word choice and verb formation.

- May use few cohesive devices.

- Shows control of present tense and near future.

- Shows control of basic vocabulary and the ability to talk about topics related to self, family, home, school, daily activities, leisure activities, personal preferences, and interests.

- Produces some variety of information.

- Shows good fluency but speech still may contain frequent pauses, repetitions, and frequent groping for words.

- May show inaccurate pronunciation of words and a strong nonnative accent.

### Intermediate High

- Shows evidence of connected discourse and emergence of organizational features.

- Produces longer sentences showing partial control of cohesive and subordinate devices.

- Shows control of present tense but uses the past tenses and the future inconsistently.

- Talks with ease about personal activities and immediate surroundings.

- Has only occasional pauses and groping for words.

- Is usually understood by native speakers unaccustomed to dealing with nonnative speakers.

*Reprinted with permission of the American Council on the Teaching of Foreign Languages.*

---

A key aspect of performance assessment is that it not only measures student performance, but also helps develop it. Grant Wiggins (1998) proposes that the performance assessment be educative in two ways.

1. It should be designed to teach by improving the performance of both teacher and learner.

2. It should evoke exemplary pedagogy. Educative assessment improves performance, does not just audit it.

Curtain and Pesola (1994) in *Languages and Children: Making the Match* advocate that teachers assess their students' ability to put their language knowledge to use in authentic performance rather than simply testing that knowledge in a drill or multiple choice quiz. Thus we see that assessment can improve performance if students have access to:

1. the criteria and standards for the tasks they need to master;

2. feedback in the attempts to master these tasks; and

3. opportunities to use the feedback to revise the work and resubmit.

## Integrated Performance Assessments from ACTFL

The American Council on the Teaching of Foreign Languages (ACTFL, 2003) designed Performance Assessment Units, now formally called Integrated Performance Assessments (IPAs), to address a national need for measuring student progress toward the attainment of the goal areas and competencies described in the national standards and the ACTFL Performance Guidelines for K–12 Learners (ACTFL, 1998).

An IPA is a theme-based assessment in which the tasks revolve around an authentic story. The IPA features three tasks, each of which reflects one of the three modes of communication—Interpretive, Interpersonal, and Presentational. Each task provides the content and skills necessary for the next task, so that the tasks are interrelated and build on one another.

## Student Feedback

If assessment is designed to improve performance, not just audit it, then assessment tasks need to be accompanied by quality feedback to students. Quality feedback needs to provide the student with information regarding his or her performance as compared to exemplars of model performance.

Students who participated in a pilot IPA program in Springfield, Massachusetts, commented that the assessment helped them to identify strengths in using the target language. They talked about increased fluency and the importance of having a broad vocabulary. Additionally, students acknowledged that access to Internet resources and references was invaluable. Students in Fairfax, Virginia, echoed these sentiments and reflected that their improvement stemmed from the assessment. Because both their strengths and weaknesses were identified, they could focus on what was necessary for better proficiency. Students felt they were challenged to achieve higher expectations for performance and therefore took greater risks with the language.

Teachers who participated in the Springfield pilot also noted that the opportunity to progress through the communication strands using authentic materials made the assessment much more realistic. Most importantly, this pilot afforded teachers the opportunity to reflect on their instruction and assessment and to recognize the IPA program as a cyclical process that advances language learning.

# Technology's Role

A foreign language teacher might ask, "How can the use of technology help to organize and contextualize good performance assessments?" Technology allows us to access current real-life print, audio, and video, establishing a realistic context for the task. It offers the opportunity to compare and contrast issues in real time by employing the different modes of communication: Interpretive, Interpersonal, and Presentational. Opportunities exist for feedback in an atmosphere that is more supportive and allows for growth. Access to technology opens the doors for presentational communication, enabling students to convey their ideas in print, audio, or video through digital presentations, WebQuests, or authentic letters to the editor.

Incorporating technology in the classroom is not only an efficient way to teach languages, but it is also an effective one. Even so, access to information, and all the possibilities surrounding that information, necessitates professional development for foreign language teachers. To improve a program, investments in professional development have to be significant. Foreign language teachers and instructional technology specialists need to come together to reflect and brainstorm the possibilities for creative language use by teachers and students. Professional development needs to focus on technology to strengthen the regular curriculum.

Schools today offer greater opportunities to use multimedia labs for random pairings in which students can practice circumlocution and modeling of real-life situations, as well as questioning techniques. This use of technology enables students to become more independent learners who are willing to take risks and express themselves in a learned language using a broader range of contexts.

# Case Study: Springfield Public Schools

The strands of assessment and technology come together in the story of the Foreign Language Department of Springfield Public Schools in Springfield, Massachusetts. In 1993, Kathy Riordan (Springfield foreign language director) and Rita Oleksak (Springfield foreign language mentor teacher) joined with other teachers and embarked on an instruction and assessment journey that continues today.

Our story includes elements of professional development, school district commitment, teacher commitment, and a shared belief in the importance of foreign language learning as part of the general curriculum. The Springfield district has more than 26,000 students, as well as 46 school buildings and 125 foreign language teachers—not a narrow scope for the task at hand.

As a team, we developed and implemented a districtwide curriculum assessment program of the elementary, middle, and senior high foreign language program. The district supported this effort with funds for curriculum and professional development workshops on the Standards for Foreign Language Learning; the ACTFL K–12 Proficiency Guidelines; the development and implementation of large-scale assessments of speaking, listening comprehension, and writing; the evaluation of the assessments; and the use of the assessment data for the improvement of student learning and future professional development for teachers.

At the beginning, we thought that we understood the full magnitude of the task before us. At each step, however, we saw greater possibilities, and the task grew even larger.

## Elementary

At the elementary school level, teachers developed, implemented, and evaluated the results of a districtwide assessment of listening comprehension for students of Chinese, French, Russian, and Spanish. The listening comprehension assessment has been in use since 1993 and has been reviewed and improved annually. For two years, teachers also implemented a speaking assessment. After the first two years, however, the speaking component became too burdensome given the large numbers of students and challenging testing conditions.

In recent years, the department added a reading assessment to the program as part of the district effort to focus on reading skills as mandated by the No Child Left Behind Act of 2001 and the state's high-stakes assessment program. This program is implemented by the foreign language teachers and uses a paper-and-pencil approach.

The director shares results and recommendations for improvement with teachers, principals, and senior district-level administrators in an annual report.

## Middle School

At the middle school level, the assessment program evolved over time. At this level, language teachers developed and implemented an annual assessment of writing and speaking in all languages offered. All Grade 8 foreign language students submitted a writing sample in the language being studied. A randomly chosen sample of students also presented an audio-recorded speech. Random sampling for the speaking component was necessary because of the limited access to technology for the administration of the assessment.

The teachers participated in professional development experiences to prepare them to evaluate the student samples. The classroom teacher ratings were used at the school level as part of the student grading process. All of the student writing and speaking samples were submitted to a districtwide team of experienced teachers and evaluators for review. These teachers reviewed samples of student work and shared their ratings with the appropriate teachers for their personal review. This process allowed all foreign language teachers to benefit from the thinking of other experienced colleagues. This is a form of teacher collaboration, although not face-to-face.

The middle school student data were reviewed and gathered with considerable time and effort. The data provided the material for the districtwide middle school report that included student results and recommendations for the improvement of instruction, professional development, and the program in general.

## High School

At the high school level, the process mirrored the assessment program at the middle school with one significant difference. All students were assessed in both speaking and writing. Most of the Springfield high schools have multimedia language centers that made possible the administration of the speaking assessment. At this level, there was much more data to manage using a paper-and-pencil process. Because no data management system was available, there were limitations in our ability to aggregate and disaggregate the data. We knew we wanted to do more with the impressive amounts of data, but we lacked the technology to make this dream happen. We had to wait until our technology capacity matched our conceptual understanding of where we wanted to go.

This old-time approach to assessment produced wonderful results, but it was highly labor intensive at both the classroom teacher level and at the administrative level. In spite of the tremendous work effort, the department as a whole believed that the assessment was essential as we worked to monitor student progress and program improvement. We also believed that the foreign language department needed to have data and hard evidence about program results just as our colleagues in other subject areas have data from standardized tests and from the high-stakes state assessment program. Understanding the importance of data-driven instruction, the Springfield foreign language teachers took on another enormous task.

## Technology to the Rescue

Springfield Public Schools embarked on a massive school-building program in the early 1990s to replace and renovate schools that were outdated given new advances in technology. All new buildings included modern technology improvements in classrooms and multimedia labs. All new middle and high schools included at least one foreign language multimedia center with the latest in technological advances. Older schools purchased wireless mobile units to address their needs. This technology upgrade paved the way for a significant leap forward in the use of technology in both the teaching and assessment of foreign languages.

The district continued to commit to teacher professional development as new technology became available. We now had the technology and were acquiring the skills to make technology work for both instruction and assessment. The district now needed some outside support and expertise in both assessment and technology.

The expertise arrived in 2002 with the partnership of the Springfield Public Schools with Language Learning Solutions (now Avant Assessment) in Eugene, Oregon. Foreign language professionals at the University of Oregon in Eugene worked with federal funds to develop a system of online foreign language assessments called the Standards-based Measurement of Proficiency (STAMP) (www.avantassessment.com/products/about_stamp.html). Beginning in 2002 and continuing today, the language teachers in the Springfield Public Schools and their colleagues at Avant Assessment have worked together to develop and implement assessments of reading and writing for foreign language students in Grade 8 and in level two in high school using an Internet-based software program. Other online assessments such as the Minnesota Language Proficiency Assessment (MLPA) and Pittsburgh Public Schools' Online World Language Testing Software (OWL Testing Software) were being developed at the time, but given the demographics of Springfield students and our need for immediate and detailed data reporting and analysis, STAMP was the best option for us. (For other assessment options, including a comparison chart, see pages 40–43.)

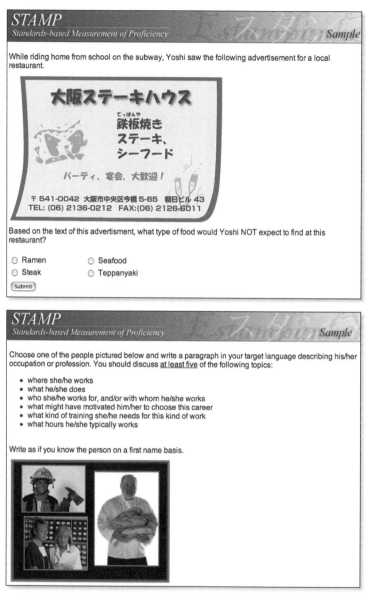

**Figure 3.1.** A STAMP reading question and a writing question.

*Reprinted with permission from the Center for Applied Second Language Studies/Avant Assessment.*

STAMP is delivered entirely online. Reading, speaking, and writing sections are available in Spanish, French, German, Japanese, Italian, and Chinese. Students begin with a computer-adaptive interpretive section (reading). Based on those interpretive scores, students are given presentational speaking or writing prompts (Figure 3.1). Student writing or speaking samples are distributed to certified graders online. Interpretive results are available immediately and presentational results within a few weeks (Figure 3.2).

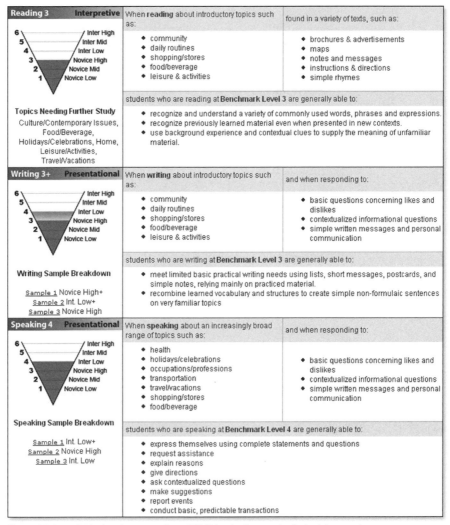

Figure 3.2. An individual student report from STAMP breaks down topics for both interpretive and presentational skills.

*Reprinted with permission from the Center for Applied Second Language Studies/Avant Assessment.*

The real power of STAMP is in the data reflected back to teachers and students. Putting performance data in the hands of practitioners has the potential to change the way we think about teaching, professional development, and student performance. The advantage of the online assessment is the ability to aggregate and disaggregate the results in multiple ways to allow teachers, students, and administrators to draw conclusions about how individuals and classes of students perform on various item types (Falsgraf, 2005). The breakdown on topics allows the teacher to adjust curriculum and improve instruction based on the data. The use of Classpak and Quizpak, language-specific instructional materials designed around the STAMP assessment, offers students multiple opportunities throughout the year to work on practice activities that are authentic and current (Falsgraf, 2005).

The STAMP assessments are administered in multimedia centers or using the wireless mobile units. The reading and writing components of the assessment program employ culturally appropriate sources for the materials. Students are interested in the content of the assessment because the materials are current; subsequently, they focus very intently on the assessment process. They are comfortable with the technology and the format of the assessment because they have used instructional materials similar to the assessment format. This classroom instruction component of the program reduces student anxiety.

This assessment program is computer adaptive to enable students to progress to their highest level of proficiency. Students begin with the reading component and with reading items until reaching their highest performance levels. Using the reading assessment results, teachers set the proficiency level for the writing assessment for each student. As a result, each student benefits from a personal and appropriate assessment in both reading and writing.

The Avant Assessment program allows the department to analyze the data in multiple ways: by class, by level, and by topic assessed. By merging the Avant Assessment data with the district student database, the department can look at student progress from grade to grade and school to school. The department can also view results using variables such as the student's grade level of initial language study, native language, ethnicity, and socioeconomic factors. The outcomes provide detailed information to identify targeted populations for which additional support is needed. The synthesis of the Avant Assessment data and the district student database has not only helped the department learn about the power of data but has also shed light on a previously untapped group of foreign language advocates—the targeted populations. In addition, the assessment data have become an essential component of the districtwide professional development program.

As is true in most districts, the assessment story in Springfield is a work in progress. The story began with the belief that a strong assessment program is essential in improving student learning. The story continues with the use of technology in foreign language instruction and in the administration and evaluation of assessments. But, most importantly, the school district's partnership with Avant Assessment offers the foreign language teachers an effective method to analyze data to improve student learning in a way only imagined in 1993.

The foreign language teachers in Springfield are continuing on this challenging journey to use technology to improve foreign language instruction through performance-based assessments. These assessments are administered and evaluated using the power of technology, and they provide the data needed to begin the dialogue to improve instruction. However, foreign language teachers should be mindful of the caution given by Jean W. LeLoup and Robert Ponteiro as stated in the *Center for Applied Linguistics Digest* (LeLoup, 2003):

> More important than the use of technology per se is the quality of what is done with this medium. A badly conceived interactive task or activity is poor whether it is done on a computer or face-to-face. Using technology is not enough. In order to promote successful learning, tasks must be meaningful, have a true interactional component, and have a comprehensible purpose for the language student (Chapelle, 1997; Liu et al., 2002; Warschauer & Healey, 1998). Future CALL [Computer Assisted Language Learning] research endeavors should begin with this premise.

We can only imagine future chapters in the Springfield story as foreign language teachers in Springfield and their partners at Avant Assessment in Oregon continue to collaborate with other colleagues around the country to realize the dream of data-driven foreign language instruction.

# Computerized Foreign Language Performance Assessment Options

While this chapter discusses the Standards-based Measurement of Proficiency (STAMP; www.avantassessment.com) in detail, other assessment options are available. Descriptions of some of these appear below along with web addresses for more information. A comparison chart follows.

## DIALANG

*www.dialang.org*

DIALANG is a European project for the development of diagnostic language tests in 14 European languages. Supported by the European Commission, these tests are computer-based and delivered on the Internet free of charge. Separate tests are available in reading, writing, listening, grammar, and vocabulary, covering all proficiency levels from beginning to advanced. Self-assessment is a key component of each test, and examinees' performance is scored based on the proficiency scales established in the Council of Europe's "Common European Framework of Reference." Instant, skill-specific feedback is provided to examinees, as well as advice on how to improve proficiency.

## MLPA

*www.carla.umn.edu/assessment/MLPA.html*

Developed by the Center for Advanced Research on Language Acquisition at the University of Minnesota, the Minnesota Language Proficiency Assessments (MLPA) are performance-based second language assessment tools for reading, writing, listening, and speaking. Currently offered in French, German, and Spanish, the MLPA are designed to measure second language proficiency levels from Intermediate Low to Intermediate High on the ACTFL Proficiency Guidelines scale. The assessments are offered in both computer-based and paper-and-pencil formats, and are equally suitable to large-group administrations or individualized testing.

## OWL Testing Software

*www.owlts.com*

Originally developed by the Pittsburgh Public Schools District, OWL Testing Software (Online World Language Testing Software) is a web-based application for authoring and administering oral proficiency examinations online. The OWL Testing Software allows language teachers to create their own performance-based assessments using images, audio, and video. Teachers can search for questions and tasks based on the ACTFL Proficiency Guidelines, and evaluate student performance using rubrics derived either from the ACTFL standards or from particular state or district foreign language standards.

## WebCAPE

*www.aetip.com/Products/CAPE/CAPE2.cfm*

Developed by Brigham Young University as a placement exam for incoming college students, WebCAPE (Web-based Computer Adaptive Placement Exam) is an Internet-based foreign language reading assessment for French, German, Russian, Spanish, ESL and Chinese. It uses adaptive technology to adjust exam difficulty to the student's proficiency level, asking a more difficult question every time the student answers the previous item correctly, and an easier question when the student misses the previous item. In this way, an accurate assessment of the examinee's proficiency can be gauged and immediate feedback offered.

## Keys to Comparison Chart

### Assessment Key

| | |
|---|---|
| **AP:** | Advanced Placement Examination |
| **CLEP:** | College Level Examination Program |
| **DIALANG:** | European system of LANGuage DIAgnosis |
| **IB Exam:** | International Baccalaureate Examination |
| **MLPA:** | Minnesota Language Proficiency Assessments |
| **MultiCAT:** | Multimedia Computer Adaptive Test |
| **OPI:** | Includes OPI—Oral Proficiency Instrument; |
| | COPI—Computerized Oral Proficiency Instrument; |
| | SOPI—Simulated Oral Proficiency Instrument |
| **OWL-TS:** | Online World Language (OWL) Testing Software |
| **SAT II:** | Scholastic Aptitude Test II |
| **STAMP:** | Standards-based Measurement of Proficiency |
| **WebCAPE:** | Web-based Computer Adaptive Placement Exam |

### Applications Key

**CR** = credit granting

**EP** = entrance placement

**EX** = exit proficiency measurement

**PE** = program evaluation

**SA** = self-assessment

## COMPARISON CHART OF COMMON LANGUAGE ASSESSMENTS

| | AP | CLEP | DIA-LANG | IB Exam | MLPA | Multi-CAT | OPI | OWL-TS | SAT II | STAMP | Web-CAPE |
|---|---|---|---|---|---|---|---|---|---|---|---|
| Available Nationally | ▪ | ▪ | ▪ | ▪ | ▪ | | ▪ | ▪ | ▪ | ▪ | ▪ |
| Web-based | | | ▪ | | | | | | | ▪ | ▪ |
| Computer Adaptive | | | | | ▪ | ▪ | | | | ▪ | ▪ |
| Statistically Validated | | ▪ | ▪ | | ▪ | | ▪ | ▪ | | ▪ | ▪ |
| Standards-based | | | ▪ | | ▪ | | ▪ | ▪ | | ▪ | |
| Proficiency-based, Culturally Authentic | | | ▪ | ▪ | ▪ | ▪ | ▪ | ▪ | | ▪ | |
| Reading Assessment | ▪ | ▪ | ▪ | ▪ | ▪ | ▪ | | | ▪ | ▪ | ▪ |
| Writing Assessment | ▪ | | ▪ | ▪ | ▪ | | | | | ▪ | |
| Speaking Assessment | ▪ | | | ▪ | ▪ | | ▪ | ▪ | | ▪ | |
| Listening Assessment | ▪ | ▪ | ▪ | ▪ | ▪ | ▪ | | | ▪ | ▪ | |
| Externally Graded with Verified Inter-rater Reliability | ▪ | ▪ | | ▪ | ▪ | ▪ | ▪ | | | ▪ | |
| Staff Development Component | ▪ | | | ▪ | ▪ | | | | | ▪ | |
| Application(s) | CR, EP | CR, EP | EP, SA | CR, EP | EP, EX | EP | EP, EX | PE | EP | EP, EX, PE | EP |

# Conclusion

In this chapter we have discussed the use of technology to improve both our instruction and our assessment, and, as a result, to provide students the opportunity to become proficient in at least one language in addition to their first so that they become full citizens of the United States and of the global society. We also shared the Springfield story, other computerized foreign language assessment options, and considered the importance of performance assessment, the use of technology to help educators organize and contextualize good performance assessments, and the relationship between performance assessment and online tests.

# References

American Council on the Teaching of Foreign Languages (ACTFL). (1986). *ACTFL proficiency guidelines*. Alexandria, VA: Author.

American Council on the Teaching of Foreign Languages (ACTFL). (1996). *Standards for foreign language learning: Preparing for the 21st century*. Alexandria, VA: Author.

American Council on the Teaching of Foreign Languages (ACTFL). (1998). *ACTFL performance guidelines for K–12 learners*. Alexandria, VA: Author.

American Council on the Teaching of Foreign Languages (ACTFL). (1999). *ACTFL proficiency guidelines: Speaking*. Retrieved from http://www.actfl.org/i4a/pages/index.cfm?pageid=3325

American Council on the Teaching of Foreign Languages (ACTFL). (2001). *ACTFL proficiency guidelines: Writing*. Retrieved from http://www.actfl.org/i4a/pages/index.cfm?pageid=3326

American Council on the Teaching of Foreign Languages (ACTFL). (2003). *ACTFL integrated performance assessment*. Alexandria, VA: Author.

Blaz, D. (2001). *A collection of performance tasks and rubrics: Foreign languages*. Larchmont, NY: Eye on Education.

Brecht, R. D., & Walton, A. R. (1994). The future shape of language learning in the new world of global communication: Consequences for higher education and beyond. In R. Donato & R. M. Terry (Eds.), *Foreign language learning: The journey of a lifetime*. Lincolnwood, IL: National Textbook Co.

Curtain, H., & Pesola, C. (1994). *Languages and children: Making the match* (2nd ed.). New York, NY: Longman.

Falsgraf, C. (2005). Reflective online assessment and empirical pedagogy. Proceedings of the 2005 Digital Stream Conference, California State University Monterey Bay, CA.

Koda, J. (1998, June). *Authentic performance assessment. In CLASS (The Center on Learning, Assessment, & School Structure). Developing authentic performance assessments.* Presentation made to ACTFL, Beyond the OPI Assessment Group, Yonkers, NY.

LeLoup, J. W., & Ponteiro, R. (2003, December). Second language acquisition and technology: A review of the research. *CAL Digest* EDO-FL-03-11.

Lewin, L., & Shoemaker, B. (1998). *Great performances: Creating classroom-based assessment tasks.* Alexandria, VA: Association for Supervision and Curriculum Development.

National Standards in Foreign Language Education Project. (1999, 2006). *Standards for foreign language learning in the 21st century* (3rd ed.). Alexandria, VA: American Council on the Teaching of Foreign Languages (ACTFL).

National Standards in Foreign Language Education Project. (n.d.). *Standards for foreign language education.* Retrieved from www.actfl.org/i4a/pages/index.cfm?pageid=3392

Pufahl, I., Rhodes, N., & Christian, D. (2004/2005, December/January). Language learning: A worldwide perspective. *Educational Leadership, 62*(4), 24–30.

Wiggins, G. (1998). *Educative assessment: Designing assessments to inform and improve student performance.* San Francisco. CA: Jossey-Bass.

# SECTION 2

# Resource Units

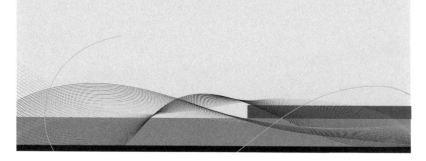

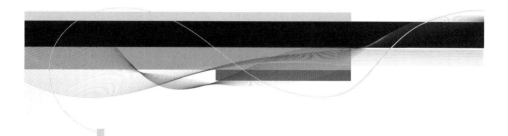

### CHAPTER 4

# CoBaLTT Project

## Content-Based Language Teaching with Technology

## Introduction

*Laurent Cammarata and Diane J. Tedick*

Who as a foreign language teacher has not dreamed of making language learning a meaningful and fun experience? Who has not thought about bringing in content related to learners' interests and experiences and imagined what that might do to the overall dynamic of the language classroom? And who as a teacher has not wanted to weave his or her own passions into the language curriculum? The foreign language curriculum can bring in so much more than language! But this is possible only if a teacher uses a curricular approach that integrates language with content that is interesting to learners. Content-based instruction (CBI) is just such a curricular approach.

CBI echoes the voices of philosophers in education, such as Rousseau and Dewey, who have emphasized the importance of developing instruction that is meaningful to the students here and now—instruction that creates bridges between subject matter content and learners' real-world experiences. CBI is also supported by the latest research in the fields of education, cognitive psychology, and second language acquisition. It has been identified as a key curricular approach in second/foreign language education (e.g., Brinton, Snow, & Wesche, 2003; Grabe & Stoller, 1997; Mohan, 1986), and it is very effective in a range of language settings, including immersion (e.g., Genesee, 1987, 1994; Johnson & Swain, 1997), English as a second language (e.g., Snow & Brinton, 1997), and more traditional foreign language contexts (e.g., Stryker & Leaver, 1997).

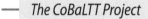

## The CoBaLTT Project

The CoBaLTT project (www.carla.umn.edu/cobaltt) was funded by the U.S. Department of Education Title VI program through the Center for Advanced Research on Language Acquisition (CARLA; www.carla.umn.edu) at the University of Minnesota. CoBaLTT staff members were Director Diane J. Tedick, Graduate Program Associate Laurent Cammarata, and Instructor and Web Weaver Marlene Johnshoy, who provided technology instruction and web support for the program.

The purpose of the Content-Based Language Teaching with Technology (CoBaLTT) professional development program is to help K–16 foreign language teachers become familiar with CBI and to provide tools to enable them to integrate this curricular approach into their teaching. The biggest challenge of weaving cognitively appropriate and meaningful content into existing foreign language teaching practice is that most curricula currently in place focus only on language (functions, grammar, vocabulary). The CoBaLTT program proposed a curricular framework that helps teachers learn how to integrate content and language.

## Other Levels and Other Languages

The two CoBaLTT units presented in this chapter were developed by teachers for specific needs, but the concepts and ideas are applicable to a wide variety of contexts and levels. The Le Moyen Âge en France unit, for example, could be adapted for use by middle school learners in immersion settings. The same themes of political, historical, and cultural change in the Middle Ages could be applied to German, Spanish, or Italian classes as well.

The program combined a year-long professional development program with support from a web resource center (www.carla.umn.edu/cobaltt/) to guide teachers through the process of planning CBI lessons and units. Through face-to-face instruction and online instructional modules the participants learned about:

- Key principles and rationales for CBI

- National standards and their relationship to CBI

- Curriculum development for CBI

- Instructional strategies for CBI

- Performance assessment for CBI

- Technological applications to support CBI

Each of these areas was taught through online instructional modules that provided readings (along with guided reading templates) and other activities for learning the concepts and supporting CBI instruction. CoBaLTT participants worked through the modules and participated in face-to-face instruction throughout the year as they developed mini CBI units. They utilized the CoBaLTT curriculum framework, which was designed to aid them in developing the units. Following a CBI curricular organization, the units included a number of lessons that explored connected topics that all relate to an overarching main theme. The CoBaLTT curriculum framework is presented in an online template that includes many help windows to guide the curriculum development process (www.carla.umn.edu/cobaltt/lessonplans/cbi_template). The templates are divided into three major sections: a unit overview section (Figure 4.1), a section for developing detailed lesson plans (Figures 4.2a, b, c), and a unit assessment section (Figure 4.3).

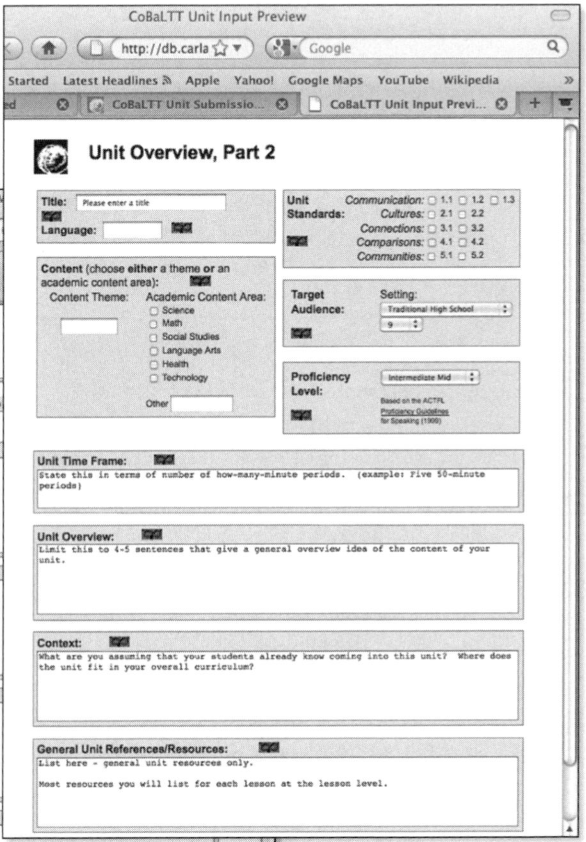

**Figure 4.1.** Example of the CoBaLTT curriculum template, Unit Overview.

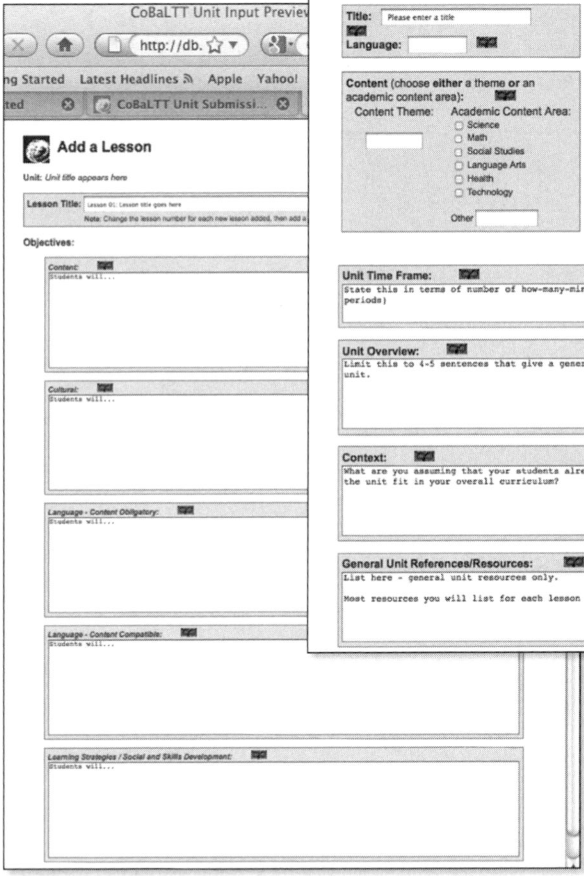

**Figure 4.2a.** Example of the CoBaLTT curriculum template, Lesson Template.

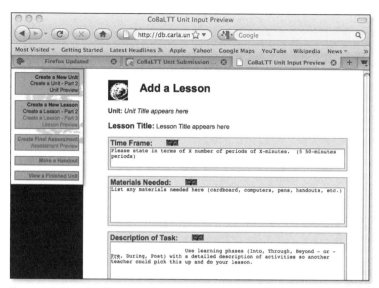

**Figure 4.2b.** Example of the CoBaLTT curriculum template, Lesson Template.

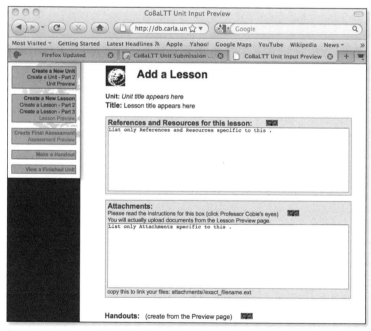

**Figure 4.2c.** Example of the CoBaLTT curriculum template, Lesson Template.

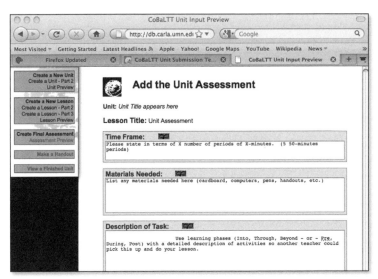

Figure 4.3. Example of the CoBaLTT curriculum template, Unit Assessment.

Complete CoBaLTT published units come with everything needed for other teachers to be able to use them right away, such as downloadable attachments of materials, activities, and assessment rubrics. The framework puts special emphasis on helping teachers develop clear objectives for each lesson of the unit. This is a departure from the focus on unit objectives in this publication. Therefore, we distinguish the two in the CoBaLTT units showcased in this volume by referring to unit goals in contrast to lesson objectives. Unit goals for both content and language are written broadly to identify the long-range aims of the unit as a whole. Lesson objectives, in contrast, are stated concretely and in detail so that teachers are clear about the content and cultural concepts they are teaching as well as the language that should be emphasized in individual lessons.

Following the framework set forth by Snow, Met, and Genesee (1989), language objectives are organized into two categories—content-obligatory (i.e., necessary for learning about the content) and content-compatible (i.e., additional language that complements the content and enhances students' language learning). Lesson objectives also highlight specific learning strategies that may be important for the lesson. To ensure that teachers successfully integrate content and language in their lessons, it is important that they write clear and precise objectives that are assessable. The CoBaLTT unit framework is quite prescriptive, as it helps teachers who are new to CBI. It also serves to provide a standard framework for every unit so that they are written in enough detail for other teachers to use. Units culminate with final performance assessment projects and accompanying rubrics to assess students' language use and content knowledge.

This volume contains one CoBaLTT unit for French for middle school students, and one for French at the high school level. The print material includes a summarized version of the unit, and the accompanying CD provides the complete version with all the necessary handouts and rubrics. We adapted these units from their original versions to incorporate an additional focus on technology. These units and others available at the website are designed to be manageable even if access to technology is not sufficient to allow for effective integration of it in the curriculum. We invite you to visit the CoBaLTT web resource center (www.carla.umn.edu/cobaltt/) to learn more about this project and about ways to integrate language and content instruction. It is free and geared toward teachers who are interested in learning more about CBI as well as teacher educators who teach about CBI.

# References

Brinton, D. M., Snow, M. A., & Wesche, M. (2003). *Content-based second language instruction* (2nd ed.). Ann Arbor, MI: University of Michigan Press.

Genesee, F. (1987). *Learning through two languages: Studies of immersion and bilingual education.* Cambridge, MA: Newbury House.

Genesee, F. (1994). *Integrating language and content: Lessons from immersion.* (Educational Practice Report No. 11). Santa Cruz, CA, and Washington, DC: National Center for Research on Cultural Diversity and Second Language Learning.

Grabe, W., & Stoller, F. L. (1997). Content-based instruction: Research foundations. In M. A. Snow & D. M. Brinton (Eds.), *The content-based classroom: Perspectives on integrating language and content* (pp. 5–21). New York, NY: Longman.

Johnson, K., & Swain, M. (1997). *Immersion education: International perspectives.* New York, NY: Cambridge University Press.

Mohan, B. A. (1986). *Language and content.* Reading, MA: Addison Wesley.

Snow, M. A., & Brinton, D. (Eds.). (1997). *The content-based classroom: Perspectives on integrating language and content.* New York, NY: Longman.

Snow, M. A., Met, M., & Genesee, F. (1989). A conceptual framework for the integration of language and context in second/foreign language instruction. *TESOL Quarterly, 23*(2), 201–216.

Stryker, S. B., & Leaver, B. L. (1997). *Content-based instruction in foreign language education: Models and methods.* Washington, DC: Georgetown University Press.

# UNIT 1

# Le Moyen Âge en France

## OVERVIEW

### AT A GLANCE

**Target Age:** High school

**Language:** French

**ACTFL Proficiency Level:** Intermediate Mid to Intermediate High

**Primary Content Area:** World history

**Connections to Other Disciplines:** Geography, architecture, art, literature, political science

**Time Frame:** 5 weeks (6 activities including Unit Assessments)

### UNIT OBJECTIVES

Students will be able to:

- Explore the history of France during the Middle Ages (about 476 to 1453 A.D.).

- Learn about major events during the Middle Ages.

- Investigate the topics of governance and leadership, challenges (war, famine, disease), and cultural and artistic creations.

- Learn about the effect of events, people, and works of literature and art on medieval society.

- Address the question of why medieval heroes and artistic creations are still considered important today.

- Understand and use the present tense and past tenses (*imparfait, passé composé,* and *passé simple*) to engage in a variety of reading, writing, and speaking activities.

- Use a variety of learning strategies to extend academic skills.

## DESCRIPTION

This unit is designed for a traditional fourth-year high school French class, including students who have studied French only in traditional classrooms as well as students who have completed an immersion program through the elementary and middle school years.

In French IV at Edina (Minnesota) High School, students use the first half of the textbook *Trésors du Temps,* by Yvone Lenard, which provides an introduction to French history from prehistoric days to the end of the 16th century. The lessons in this unit utilize and enhance the materials in *Trésors du Temps.* During the course of this unit, students explore the history of France during the Middle Ages (about 476 to 1453 A.D.). As they learn about major events during this time frame, they investigate the topics of governance and leadership, challenges (war, famine, disease), and cultural and artistic creations. They learn about the effect of events, people, and works of literature and art on medieval society, and address the question of why medieval heroes and artistic creations are still considered important today.

## STANDARDS ADDRESSED

### NETS·S

- Creativity and Innovation 1.a, 1.b

- Communication and Collaboration 2.a, 2.b, 2.c, 2.d

- Research and Information Fluency 3.b, 3.c

- Critical Thinking, Problem Solving, and Decision Making 4.a, 4.b

- Technology Operations and Concepts 6.b

**Standards for Foreign Language Learning**

- Communication Standards 1.1, 1.2, 1.3

- Cultures Standards 2.1, 2.2

- Connections Standards 3.1, 3.2

- Communities Standard 5.1

## CONNECTIONS TO OTHER DISCIPLINES

Topics in geography, architecture, art, literature, and political science can all be explored through the content introduced in this unit. Each of these content areas is easily and naturally connected to the study of history. It is difficult to imagine, in fact, how students could learn about the Middle Ages in France without knowing something about the geography of medieval Europe or the geopolitical tensions at play at the time. Art and scripture were the two major means used to record knowledge during the Middle Ages, so they become important domains in this unit. The evolution of architecture and the building of cathedrals—projects that often lasted hundreds of years and involved generations of builders—represent an observable trace of the incredible social transformation that marked the transition between the Dark Ages and the Renaissance.

## SPOTLIGHT ON TECHNOLOGY

**Web Browsers and Asynchronous Communication Software.** The Internet has opened many new possibilities that are particularly meaningful to teachers who want to implement CBI. It provides endless access to authentic materials, one of the biggest challenges identified by CBI instructors. Using e-mail, chat, and instant messaging, students can also go beyond the limited communication that occurs within the classroom environment and connect with experts and native speakers to gather information regarding particular topics.

**Word Processing Software.** Word processing software such as Word or Google Docs can provide an opportunity for students to work on newsletters and journals for publication. Publishing brings another dimension to learning, as it gives students an opportunity to communicate to real audiences for meaningful purposes. Google Docs allows students to work collaboratively; students in separate locations on separate computers may all access a single document at the same time.

**Concept Mapping Software.** Concept mapping software such as Inspiration can expand learners' ability to conceptualize and organize their knowledge, and can help them outline and plan more complex oral and written projects—an important academic skill for all content areas. Because this software requires learners to visually map their thinking processes, it can also help support different intelligences and learning styles.

**Multimedia Authoring Tools.** Using computer technology can increase opportunities for creation and expression. If computers are available and loaded with appropriate presentation software such as PowerPoint or Google Presentations, students can integrate images, music, and other multimedia elements from the Internet into their work. Focusing on presenting for a particular audience and making information clear and appealing is a skill that high school students should practice extensively, because they will benefit from it in the future.

**Wikis.** Wikis serve as a resource repository and reference on a particular topic and are particularly suited to group work and collaboration. Wikis can store vocabulary words, timelines, lists of facts, and examples of student work, and they allow the students themselves to do the creation, editing, and maintenance.

## TECHNOLOGY RESOURCES NEEDED

### Hardware

- computers with Internet access (optional)
- overhead or LCD projector, or interactive white board
- web space on a server, or use Google Sites (optional)

### Software

- Internet browsing and e-mail capabilities (optional)
- word processing software (optional)
- concept mapping software such as Inspiration (optional)
- multimedia authoring tools such as PowerPoint or Google Presentations (optional)
- access to a wiki (optional)

## SUPPLEMENTARY RESOURCES

### Web Resources

De la fortification: http://sabreteam.free.fr/fortif2.htm

Liens vers des sites sur le Moyen Âge:
http://his.nicolas.free.fr/Histoire/Liens/LiensHMAge.html

Le Moyen Âge:
http://his.nicolas.free.fr/Histoire/Panorama/MoyenAge/MoyenAge

Un voyage de plusieurs siècles en Gaule:
http://jean-francois.mangin.pagesperso-orange.fr

### Literature Resources

Barroy, M.-H. (1984). *L'histoire de France par les mots croisés.* Paris, France: Éditions Retz.

Caselli, G. (1981). *La vie privée des hommes: Le Moyen Âge.* Paris, France: Hachette Livre.

Caselli, G. (1998). *La vie privée des hommes: Des Celtes aux chevaliers du Moyen Âge.* Paris, France: Hachette Jeunesse.

Chamot, A. U., Barnhardt, S., El-Dinary, P. B., & Robbins, J. (1999). *The learning strategies handbook.* White Plains, NY: Addison Wesley Longman.

Gibbons, P. (2002). *Scaffolding language, scaffolding learning.* Portsmouth, NH: Heinemann.

Lenard, Y. (1997). *Trésors du temps.* New York, NY: Glencoe/McGraw-Hill.

Mathiex, J. (1981). *Outils: Histoire de France.* Paris, France: Hachette Livre.

Miquel, P. (1983). *La vie privée des hommes: Histoire des Français.* Paris, France: Hachette Livre.

Nembrini, J.-L. (1996). *Histoire.* Paris, France: Hachette Livre.

# TEACHING THE UNIT

The following section provides a brief synopsis of each activity. A more detailed description of the lesson activities, formative assessment strategies, and handouts are provided on the accompanying CD.

## INTRODUCTION AU MOYEN ÂGE EN FRANCE
*Activity 1 (Days 1–3)*

### Preview

To facilitate the introduction of this theme, begin by focusing on building background, an instructional strategy that is key to developing effective content-based units. First, organize the class into groups of four students. To help learners connect their background knowledge to the topic, access students' prior knowledge about the Middle Ages in France by asking them to brainstorm in groups answers to the following question: What do you know about the Middle Ages in terms of leaders and governance, challenges, cultural and artistic products, and values and beliefs?

Encourage groups to share their ideas with the class, and have a class secretary place the ideas on large poster paper or a shared, projected wiki page. This will help the class establish a lexicon with key terminology, which will be written on a separate poster or wiki page (this will target the content obligatory language objectives set for the lesson—see the CD for a detailed description). Add words to the list throughout the course of the unit.

A variation for teachers with access to computers and concept mapping software such as Inspiration is described on the CD.

### Focused Learning

This task requires students to find dates that correspond with particular events and then place this information on a timeline. Indicate chapters in textbooks and websites where students can locate the information. To complete this task, students must copy their information onto a timeline. When done, have students share their findings with the class in an oral presentation.

### Expansion

Students will use a graphic organizer to categorize the information on the timeline. The categories are political and religious leaders, challenges, and artistic and cultural creations (Figure 4.4; Activity 1 Handout 3).

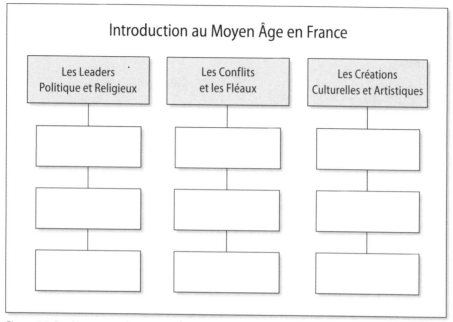

**Figure 4.4.** Graphic organizer for Le Moyen Âge en France.

After students have completed their graphic organizers, lead a discussion that explores the following questions:

- What is the relationship between the three categories? (*Quel est le rapport entre les leaders, les conflits et les fléaux tels que la guerre et la peste, et les creations artistiques?*)

- In your opinion, given the constant wars and other challenges, what were the responsibilities of medieval leaders? (*À votre avis, étant donné les guerres continuelles et les autres conflits/épreuves de l'époque, quelle était la responsabilité des leaders au Moyen Âge?*)

## Teaching Tips

Many variations of this activity are possible, depending on the knowledge base and reading level of the students. The most useful strategy to help students understand the reading has proven to be student skits or videos, including props, a narrator, and a written summary. Skits and videos can be done at any time during the unit, even throughout the unit, to enhance understanding.

## LES CONFLITS ET LES FLÉAUX AU MOYEN ÂGE
*Activity 2 (Days 4–8)*

### Preview

The lesson begins with a review of the list of challenges established during the Expansion phase of Activity 1. You may wish to display Handout 1 at this time. Have students speculate on possible causes and effects for these challenges. Note the discussion points on an overhead transparency or projected wiki page (or have a student do so).

### Focused Learning

Divide the students into groups of four and distribute Handout 1. Assign each group a topic to research (chosen randomly from this list of challenges). If computers are available, dedicate some class time to online research. Encourage students to explore historical websites to research their topic. Students will use their findings to complete a graphic organizer and write a one-paragraph summary in the past tense (using Activity 2 Handout 2; Figure 4.5).

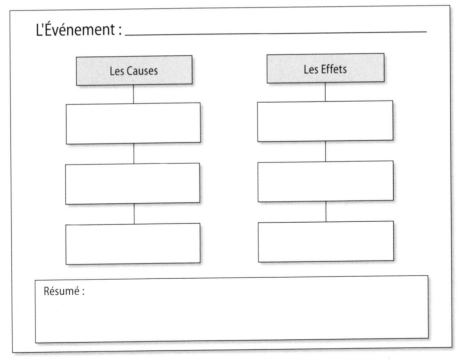

Figure 4.5. The challenges of the Middle Ages: Handout for graphic organizer and one-paragraph summary.

This task culminates in a jigsaw activity that requires students to re-form in different groups. Within the new groups, one member of each of the previous groups will present to the others. Following the presentations, have each group identify similarities and differences among the events described and answer this question: Why was this event a challenge for people living in the Middle Ages in France? (*Pourquoi est-ce que cet événement représentait une épreuve pour les Français au Moyen Âge?*)

### Expansion

Ask a speaker from each group to present the group's list of similarities and differences as well as the group's answer to the discussion question. Then have the class brainstorm a list of current events that have similar causes or effects. An extension that incorporates the use of technology is described on the accompanying CD.

### Teaching Tips

As a variation for this activity, the entire group could work on a single event, such as the plague or the 100 Years' War. Students should work first in small groups, and then share their knowledge with the class as the teacher makes notes on the graphic organizer using an overhead or projected wiki page.

## LA FÉODALITÉ
*Activity 3 (Days 9–12)*

### Preview

Begin class with a discussion of this question: What do you know about feudalism in medieval France? (*Que savez-vous de la féodalité en France au Moyen Âge?*) Note the ideas on a large sheet of paper or projected wiki page. In the course of this conversation, introduce relevant content obligatory vocabulary. See the CD for a detailed description of the lesson's objectives.

### Focused Learning

For the first task, students will read several texts describing the structure of feudalism, a fortified castle, and life in a castle in the Middle Ages. They may also read a text about knights, if you wish to also assign this. These texts are provided as Handouts 1 and 2 on the accompanying CD. Students will gain language practice during the course of this task by answering questions about the text, writing definitions for words, and rewriting sentences using different tenses. These reading and writing exercises may be completed over a period of several days. Students will also search for images and descriptions of *châteaux forts* (fortified castles) on the Internet.

For the second task, in class over a period of two days (fewer or more as needed), students in groups of four will complete the following:

- Self-correct the verbs they have written in the imperfect tense. The teacher will display text with verbs in the imperfect tense.

- Read the texts aloud with verb changes.

- Read and discuss the answers to the questions and the definitions of the words they have previously written.

## Expansion

After the two tasks have been completed, hold a class discussion (or divide the class into two or three discussion groups). Review the challenges of the Middle Ages explored in Activity 2. Prompt students with questions, such as: How did feudal society and the fortified castle help people meet those challenges? What are some similarities and differences between the role of government and leaders in the Middle Ages and the present?

As an assessment, ask student groups to create a graphic organizer on a large sheet of paper (or using graphic organizing software or a shared wiki) to explain how society was organized during the Middle Ages. Have groups present their results to the class.

As a homework assignment, ask students to write a paragraph explaining how feudal society and châteaux forts helped people meet the challenges of life in the Middle Ages. Instruct them also to analyze the disadvantages of this governance model.

## Teaching Tips

A classroom blog is a great way to share student writing and give students immediate and varied feedback from their peers.

## DES CRÉATIONS ARTISTIQUES AU MOYEN ÂGE
*Activity 4 (Days 13–17)*

### Preview

Begin the lesson with a brainstorming session in which students explore possible answers to the following questions:

- What are some examples of different types of artistic creations? (Examples include books, such as *Harry Potter*; movies, such as *Twilight*; and paintings, such as *Monet's Water Lilies*.)

- Why do people create art? (Possible answers include for personal expression, to entertain, to instruct, and to celebrate the actions of a famous person.)

- What is the role of art in a society?

List student answers on a large sheet of paper or on a projected wiki.

### Focused Learning

Divide students into groups of three to five and distribute a list of skit ideas and resources (Handout 1). Assign a topic from the list or allow groups to choose their own. Then distribute a description of the task and a checklist (Handout 2). Have students research their topic. If computers are available (or a session in a computer lab can be scheduled), have students search the Internet for images of medieval art work. Students will then be required to prepare and deliver a dramatic presentation to acquaint the class with their art piece as well as the role and importance of this cultural or artistic creation for society then and now. Distribute the skit rubric (Handout 3), so students will know what is expected of them.

Ideally, the presentation would be prepared and performed with the help of presentation software such as PowerPoint or Google Presentations, or consider allowing students to create a video or synthesize a new video by remixing existing digital video clips. Students may begin the task of gathering the material in class and then complete the presentation or video outside class as a group homework assignment.

### Expansion

Lead a summary discussion, prompting students with this question: During a time when famine, the plague, wars, and invasions affected the daily lives of people, how did artistic creations improve people's lives?

### Teaching Tips

It is interesting to expand this question to the present as well: How do artistic creations enrich our lives today?

## LA VIE DE CHARLEMAGNE
*Activity 5 (Days 18–20)*

### Preview

Begin the lesson by asking students what they already know about kings and emperors to activate their background knowledge: What is a king? What is an emperor? What is the difference? Review with the class your previous discussions about the role of leaders in the Middle Ages and record (or ask a student to record) these ideas on chart paper or a wiki page. As a final point of discussion, ask students what they already know about Emperor Charlemagne of France.

After the discussion, introduce the following homework assignment: students will read about the life of Charlemagne in the textbook *Trésors du Temps*. This will provide the necessary background for the following day's work. Students will be required to write down five main ideas from the text to share with their group the following day.

### Focused Learning

This phase of the activity has two parts: a presentation of key vocabulary terms and a dictogloss exercise. The whole class will first participate in the development of a vocabulary list, and then students will listen to and reconstruct the dictogloss text. These tasks are explained in great detail on the CD.

### Expansion

The lesson concludes with a discussion in which students review and reflect on the facts of Charlemagne's life. This will help students prepare for the final assessment activity of the unit, which is to deliver a presentation about an important historical figure from the Middle Ages. The task requires students to work in small groups to discuss various questions about Charlemagne (available in detail in French in Activity 5, Handout 2 on the CD). Assign roles, such as recorder, speaker, task facilitator/timekeeper, and language coordinator. The recorder takes notes for the group. Following the small group work, the whole class discusses the questions. First, ask the speaker from each group to present the group's response to one of the questions, and then encourage the class to add comments.

### Teaching Tips

Some students find this reading exercise to be quite challenging, so you may wish to have them use a pre-reading strategy to help with their comprehension. For instance, before beginning the Focused Learning, ask students to scan the textbook passage quickly to find the main points.

## UNIT EXTENSION AND TEACHING TIPS

### Unit Extension Activities

Have students discuss their personal concept of a hero: what qualities and/or actions make someone a hero? Have them give examples of personal heroes who are well known (e.g., Martin Luther King) as well as people they know well who are heroes for them (e.g., a parent or grandparent). Have students discuss these issues in small groups (four or five per group), followed by a large group discussion. Have each group create a list of characteristics of people they admire. Finally, ask students to write an essay describing a person they admire.

## Unit Teaching Tips

Be flexible! Don't hesitate to adapt every lesson to the needs of your students. Keep students accountable for all the work they do. Use student skits to encourage and increase understanding. Incorporate games to help students retain vocabulary, dates, and other information. This is a vast topic, so don't hesitate to pare down the material and activities to suit the needs of your class.

# ASSESSING THE UNIT

## UNIT ASSESSMENT
*Activity 6 (Days 21–27)*

### Description of Task

The final assessment of this unit is in the form of a culminating project, a type of assessment that places emphasis on the learning process and that is particularly well suited to CBI because it involves synthesis of content knowledge and language use in multiple modalities. For this task, students will be required to demonstrate knowledge of a key figure from the Middle Ages by introducing themselves as that person and presenting that historical figure's background and importance. They will answer the question "Why am I remembered today?" In answering this question, they will describe the person's life and accomplishments. If possible, they will do their presentations in the context of a school event to which other classes are invited, or as a digital video to be shared.

Students will choose their historical figure (or names may be drawn at random) from a list provided by the teacher (Handout 1). They will then spend several days in class working on the research and writing. The remainder of the research and writing will be done at home.

Students will use the description of the project, checklist, and rubrics for the oral and written presentations to complete this task (Handouts 2, 3, and 4). They will hand in the written version of their presentation, and deliver their completed speeches to the class.

Finally, students will take a multiple-choice quiz put together by the teacher from questions prepared by the presenters.

## Technology Alternatives

The final presentation could be prepared and performed with the help of software such as PowerPoint or Google Presentations. One possibility is for students to conduct their research and gather their presentation material in a computer lab. If you decide to incorporate technology in your lesson plan, use the Rubric for Assessment of NETS•S: Technology Use for Final Project (Appendix A and CD) to evaluate this use.

Also, you may encourage students to use asynchronous and synchronous communication (e-mail, instant messaging, Skype, videoconferencing) to contact experts in the field (historians, scholars, etc.) or to post questions on specialized web discussion boards. Include this in the rubric (under 2. Communication and Collaboration) as a chance to gain extra points for the zealous students who always want to do more. All traces of communication will need to be recorded and presented to the teacher as proof that such attempts were made. You may wish to reward any attempts, successful or not, but give maximum points only to exchanges that resulted in the student receiving useful information.

Finally, consider publishing the final projects online (e.g., place them on the school server, if available) to be shared with others and to stimulate future projects by modeling exemplary work.

## Unit Teaching Tips

There are several things you can do to manage this process effectively. If possible, deliver a model presentation of a historical figure to help the students visualize exactly what is expected. As they begin their work, set clear deadlines for each step of the process. In addition, remind students not to cut and paste from the Internet. They need to put all information into their own words and use citations. You could also allow students to do the project in pairs, with one student interviewing the historical figure. Remind students that they may not read their presentations, but must perform them.

## Assessment Criteria

Have students complete checklists as a self-assessment. Use the rubrics to evaluate their performance. Rubrics for the assessment tasks in this unit are provided on the accompanying CD as well as in Appendix A:

- Rubric for Oral Presentation
- Rubric for Written Version of Presentation
- Rubric for Assessment of NETS•S—Technology Use for Final Project

***Note:*** *Skit Rubric for Unit 1 is Unit 1 Activity 4, Handout 3.*

# UNIT 2

# Les Stéréotypes des Français

## OVERVIEW

### AT A GLANCE

**Target Age:** Middle school

**Language:** French

**ACTFL Proficiency Level:** Intermediate Low to Intermediate Mid

**Primary Content Area:** Cultural studies

**Connections to Other Disciplines:** Social studies and psychology

**Time Frame:** Eight 40-minute class periods; several 20-minute homework assignments (5 activities including the Unit Assessment)

### UNIT OBJECTIVES

Students will be able to:

- Develop an awareness of how preconceived notions affect the way human beings live and experience the world they inhabit.

- Reflect on the many ways that stereotypes are created and maintained.

- Develop a sensitivity to issues related to cultural diversity and become more aware of the many prejudices that we human beings all carry within us.

- Identify common stereotypes Americans hold regarding other cultures and explore their insidious remodeling of actual realities.

- Use the present tense and past tenses (*passé composé* and *imparfait*) to engage in a variety of reading, writing, and speaking activities.

- Use a range of learning strategies to organize information, work cooperatively, and expand critical thinking skills.

## DESCRIPTION

This unit is intended for a traditional fourth-year middle school French class. These fourth-year students are typically in the eighth grade and have completed the equivalent of one year of high school French. This means that they have mastered much general and basic survival vocabulary, including colors, numbers, clothing, food, geographical terms, and parts of the body, the house, and the town. They can recognize simple cognates. They can write sentences in the present tense without much prompting. They are familiar with grammatical concepts central to basic French, such as gendered nouns, subject/verb agreement, adjective agreement, and correct word order.

This unit comprises four major lessons, which are distinct yet cumulative. In Activity 1, the students lay the groundwork for their examination of French stereotypes by generating those stereotypes themselves. They may draw, write, or find examples of what they think are "typical" French things. In Activity 2, they are required to change perspective—instead of being the examiners, they are the examined culture. Students look at various stereotypes of Americans, as shown through websites and books about Americans. Thus, in Activity 2, they begin to examine stereotypes and their relationship with truth. In Activity 3, they shift again to the role of examiners of French culture—the teacher shows movies, books, pictures, and websites that might reflect the same stereotypes the students generated in Activity 1. This lesson will demonstrate concretely to the students that the image they have of French people is created and maintained by strong forces in American culture. In Activity 4, learners explore those French stereotypes in more detail in order to understand their origins and relationships with daily life and reality in France today. These lessons culminate in a final multimedia presentation project in which small groups of students working collaboratively examine a cultural myth, a generalization, and a cultural reality of French people and show their relationship to French society today.

## STANDARDS ADDRESSED

### NETS·S

- Creativity and Innovation 1.a, 1.b

- Communication and Collaboration 2.a, 2.b, 2.c, 2.d

- Research and Information Fluency 3.a, 3.b, 3.c

- Critical Thinking, Problem Solving, and Decision Making 4.a, 4.b, 4.d

- Digital Citizenship 5.b

- Technology Operations and Concepts 6.a, 6.b

### Standards for Foreign Language Learning

- Communication Standards 1.1, 1.2, 1.3

- Cultures Standards 2.1, 2.2

- Connections Standards 3.1, 3.2

- Comparisons Standard 4.2

- Communities Standard 5.1

## CONNECTIONS TO OTHER DISCIPLINES

In this unit, students explore their own views toward the French and other nationalities' views toward Americans, connecting their learning to the discipline of *social studies*. These lessons delve into issues of cultural and social identity: What does it mean to be French? What does it mean to be American? Students will be led toward the understanding that within every culture lies tremendous individual variation. This unit can, therefore, serve as a logical trampoline to explore threads related to the field of *cross-cultural psychology*, which focuses on the intricate link between individual behavior and the cultural context within which it occurs, as well as on the diversity of human behavior.

## SPOTLIGHT ON TECHNOLOGY

**Web Browsers.** Students will use the Internet to explore questions about the origins of various stereotypes as well as to utilize the many reference materials available online to clarify terms with which they might not be familiar. More advanced students can seek out online French-language publications and sources that address French and American stereotypes.

**TrackStar.** TrackStar (http://trackstar.4teachers.org) allows teachers to easily compile a list of resources for students to access online. It is designed to help students explore a variety of sites related to a particular topic, and can be used as the starting point for online lessons and activities. Using this resource, teachers can collect websites, enter them into TrackStar, and add annotations for their students in order to create interactive online lessons called *Tracks*. This online resource allows teachers to either create their own Track or use one of the hundreds of thousands already made by other educators, which are accessible online free of charge. Teachers can search the database by subject, grade, or theme and standard.

**Word Processing Software.** Word processing software such as Word or Google Docs can provide an opportunity for students to work on newsletters and journals for publication. Publishing brings another dimension to learning, as it gives students an opportunity to communicate to real audiences for meaningful purposes.

**Multimedia Authoring Tools and Web Publishing Software.** Students will create a multimedia presentation that will be shared with others in the classroom, and can be published online, using software such as PowerPoint, HyperStudio, or Google Presentations. This activity will help learners develop skills in technology, language, and cooperative work.

**Asynchronous and Synchronous Communication Software.** Using e-mail, instant messaging, chat, and videoconferencing, students can go beyond the limited communication that occurs within the classroom environment and connect with others to gather information regarding particular topics.

**Wikis.** Wikis serve as a resource repository and reference on a particular topic and are particularly suited to group work and collaboration. Wikis can store vocabulary words, timelines, lists of facts, and examples of student work, and they allow the students themselves to do the creation, editing, and maintenance.

## TECHNOLOGY RESOURCES NEEDED

### Hardware

- computers with Internet access
- television with videocassette or DVD player, or gather appropriate YouTube clips

### Software

- Internet browsing software
- TrackStar (free online software)
- word processing software
- presentation software such as PowerPoint, HyperStudio, or Google Presentations
- web publishing software such as Google Sites (optional)
- e-mail, instant messaging, chat, or videoconferencing capabilities (optional)
- access to a wiki (optional)

## SUPPLEMENTARY RESOURCES

### Information on Stereotypes

Dynamique interculturelle et stereotypes:
www.mediation-interculturelle.com/IMG/pdf/TXT-Stereotypes.pdf
Although likely to be too advanced for middle school students, this website serves as an excellent resource for teachers of French and for more advanced learners. It provides information in French about stereotypes.

Nationalities and Their Stereotypes:
http://iteslj.org/Lessons/Counihan-Stereotypes

TrackStar lesson on French stereotypes (type in track number 28811):
http://trackstar.4teachers.org/trackstar/

### Articles in English about French Culture and News

About.com: http://gofrance.about.com

U.S. News and World Report: www.usnews.com

### French Newspapers

Le Journal Français: www.france-amerique.com

Le Monde: www.lemonde.fr

L'Express: www.lexpress.fr

Libération: www.liberation.com

Paris Match: www.parismatch.com

## French Television Broadcasts

France 2: www.france2.fr

France 3: www.france3.fr

France 4: www.france4.fr

France 5: www.france5.fr

RFO: www.rfo.fr

TF1: www.tf1.fr

## French Webcams

La Chaîne Météo: www.lachainemeteo.com

TF1: http://webcams.tf1.fr

## Learning Tools

TrackStar (free online software): http://trackstar.4teachers.org/trackstar/

## Literature Resources

Faul, S. (1999). *Xenophobe's guide to the Americans.* London, England: Oval Books.

National Standards in Foreign Language Education Project. (2006). *Standards for foreign language learning in the 21st century* (3rd ed.). Alexandria, VA: American Council on the Teaching of Foreign Languages (ACTFL).

National Standards in Foreign Language Education Project. (n.d.). *Standards for foreign language education.* Retrieved from www.actfl.org/i4a/pages/index.cfm?pageid=3392

Short, D. (1993). Assessing integrated language and content instruction. *TESOL Quarterly, 27*(4), 627–647.

Yapp, N., & Syrett, M. (1999). *Xenophobe's guide to the French.* London, England: Oval Books.

# TEACHING THE UNIT

The following section provides a brief synopsis of each activity. A more detailed description of the lesson activities, formative assessment strategies, and handouts is provided on the accompanying CD.

## STEREOTYPE SIMULATION
*Activity 1 (Days 1–2)*

### Preview

On the first day of the unit, have students complete a checklist to self-assess their knowledge of web technology applications (the checklist is provided as Handout 1 on the accompanying CD). Then begin the lesson with a blank piece of paper and a pencil in the hands of each student (or a blank document open on a computer). Instruct the students to close their eyes and imagine a typical French person in their heads. Then ask some guiding questions to help learners explore their stereotypes of the French (e.g., What do typical French people usually wear?).

Once you have covered the physical appearance of French people, turn to their surroundings. Where are these "typical French people"? What possessions do they have with them? What are they doing? For an example of what this brainstorming process produced in one class session see Handout 2 on the CD.

### Focused Learning

After the image has been formed, have students document everything they have imagined about the typical French person. If the students finish early, they can draw a picture of the person as well.

The students should then reveal their work and see how many people produced similar descriptions. Any shared items of description should be put on the board or onto a shared, projected wiki, with the teacher translating into French as needed. Then introduce students to the concept of stereotype and explain that it often refers to commonly held perceptions of a people or a culture.

Next, on another section of the board or another page of the wiki, ask students more specific impressions about the French (e.g., Where do they work? Where do they live? What are some hobbies?).

## Expansion

On the next day of class, begin the final task of the lesson, organizing the stereotypes into the *Guide d'analyse des stéréotypes* chart (Activity 1 Handout 3; Figure 4.6). This chart is organized in an eight-cell 3 x 3 grid with the following categories: products, practices, and perspectives; and positive, negative, and neutral. Carefully explain each area to the students. Students should then, as you circulate the room, try to fit each of the stereotypes listed the previous day into the chart. For example, the stereotype of the French smoking all the time would be *negative* and *practice*. France associated with good food would be *positive* and *product*.

Have students start this handout in class and finish it for homework. Collect, grade, and keep this sheet to hand back during Activity 3: America Views France.

## Teaching Tips

The brainstorming session on the first day of the activity can provide interesting insights into the students and how they perceive other cultures. A student in one class defended passionately the fact that French people were known for their use of gondolas, and this after a year of French study! It also lends insight into the motivations of some students in studying French; stylish girls usually picture their typical French person as a model decked out in the latest styles; a snowboarder once imagined snowboarders in the Alps; one rap aficionado imagined a rapper!

### Guide d'analyse des stéréotypes

|  | Positif | Négatif | Neutre |
|---|---|---|---|
| Produits |  |  |  |
| Pratiques |  |  |  |
| Perspectives |  |  |  |

Figure 4.6. Handout for analyzing stereotypes.

## STEREOTYPES OF AMERICANS
*Activity 2 (Day 3)*

### Preview

Begin this lesson with a collective reading of excerpts from the book *Xenophobe's Guide to the Americans* (Faul, 1999). This English book is one of a series that claims on the cover to take "an irreverent look at the beliefs and foibles of nations, almost guaranteed to cure Xenophobia." Nonetheless, the book does reflect some common stereotypes about Americans, without being overly negative or disparaging. In beginning this lesson with a group reading, steer students in the direction of constructive commentary. The sections entitled "Attitudes and Values," "Eating and Drinking," and "Leisure and Pleasure" should all elicit appropriate reactions. If this book is unavailable, similar documents may be used. The first link of the TrackStar on French stereotypes listed below can be a suitable replacement.

### Focused Learning

After students have completed the reading, have the class collectively discuss their impressions of the text and the stereotypes described within, with each student sharing his or her thoughts in French. This initial guided discussion should adjourn to the computer lab, where students will log on to the TrackStar lesson on French stereotypes (Figure 4.7). To do so, instruct the students to access http://trackstar.4teachers.org/trackstar/ and type in track number 28811.

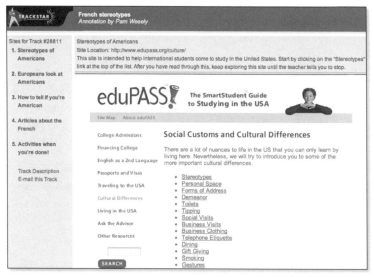

**Figure 4.7.** The TrackStar lesson on stereotypes.

The first link is a set of instructions given to foreign students planning to study in the United States. This is a very unbiased and fair document, and it is included to reinforce (or replace!) the comments in *Xenophobe's Guide to Americans*. After students have explored the first site, they should (on a cue from the teacher) move on to the second link. This link is much more controversial, and students may have more of a reaction to it. At this point, distribute another *Guide d'analyse des stéréotypes* (Activity 2 Handout 1) to the students and encourage them to fill it out using the stereotypes of Americans listed on the second site. Once they have finished the task, they should continue to the third link, which is another set of stereotypes of Americans (and the French and Australians), which they can also add to their chart. By the end of the class period, they should try to have every box on the chart filled with at least one stereotype.

## Expansion

The final task in this lesson is a discussion of stereotypes and their relationship with the truth. Once students are back in the classroom, have them look at the American *Guide d'analyse des stéréotypes*, which they just filled out. They should then attempt to categorize each stereotype into one of three categories, based on their interpretation of its relationship with the truth: a cultural myth (it is not true at all, or it is no longer true), a generalization (it is true maybe for some members of the culture but not for all), and a cultural reality (it is pretty much true for all members of the culture). Instruct students to underline or highlight the stereotypes in three different colors to reference the three categories. Have the class collectively discuss their categorizations. Encourage students to express their agreement or disagreement, and to provide reasons to support their opinions. At the end of this lesson, collect, grade, and keep this sheet.

## Teaching Tips

More mature students might be able to start this lesson with a brainstorming exercise similar to that used for the French in Activity 1. This is not recommended for younger students, however, because they are probably not aware of stereotypes of Americans and would find this exercise frustrating.

Students may be argumentative about, horrified by, or begrudgingly accepting of the stereotypes about Americans that are discussed. This activity in particular seems to heighten student awareness of cultural stereotypes, and some students may even become "experts" on the topic.

## AMERICA VIEWS FRANCE
*Activity 3 (Day 4)*

### Preview

The preview for this lesson is a student assignment. First, hand back to students their *Guide d'analyse des stéréotypes* for the French (from Activity 1). Then send students out to find examples of stereotypes of the French in the American media, particularly ones that reflect items from their *Guide d'analyse*. Prompt them by mentioning Disney movies, Warner Brothers cartoons, television commercials, or shows in which French is spoken or the French people are portrayed. Each student must find at least one good example (a plethora of appropriate articles and videos are available online). Give them several days to complete this assignment, during which time other classroom work can be undertaken.

### Focused Learning

Once examples have been collected, have students informally present the images they found of the French in the American media. During and after their presentations, have the class fill out the *Présentations* worksheet (Activity 3 Handout 1; Figure 4.8), which will assure their attention and their analysis.

| Présentations | | | | |
|---|---|---|---|---|
| **Éleve** | **Origine** | **Description** | **Classification** | **Commentaire** |
| | | | | |
| | | | | |
| | | | | |

Figure 4.8. Handout 1, *Présentations*.

In order to do this sheet, they will need to keep their French *Guide d'analyse* nearby. After these presentations, round out the examples with any images you have collected. Pass back the students' original image of the "typical French person" from Activity 1. Each student should mark on the *Présentations* handout how many of the American images are mirrored on their original "typical" sheet.

### Expansion

As a follow-up activity, discuss with the class reasons why the parallels between their personal stereotypes and the portrayal of the French in the American media exist. Collect three things at the end of the lesson: the "typical French person" brainstorming list from Activity 1, the *Guide d'analyse* of the French, and the *Présentations* sheet.

### Teaching Tips

For this activity, you could require the students to find more than one example of a stereotype of the French. You could then refrain from presenting any examples yourself, and make the exchange and discussion more student-centered and student-run.

## TRUTH AND STEREOTYPES
*Activity 4 (Days 5–8)*

### Preview

Before class, select several video news clips for student viewing (see the CD or *Supplementary Resources* for Unit 2 on pages 75–76). Then have students watch the clips on their computers and rank them on a piece of paper (or on a projected, shared wiki) in order of "Frenchness." This exercise will introduce students to the idea that some stereotypes are indeed visible and important in France, although other images and beliefs exist as well.

As a variation on this activity, ask students to explore and rank either TF1 webcam feeds (http://webcams.tf1.fr/webcam/) or La Chaîne Météo webcam feeds (www. lachainemeteo.com). You could also ask students to explore French websites and try to identify those that seem to be typical of France and those that seem atypical. Even if such an activity isn't as dynamic or interesting as watching videos, it still remains a practical alternative that can yield similar language learning experiences, especially during this phase of the lesson.

### Focused Learning

This task engages students in analyzing French stereotypes. To do this, redistribute their *Guide d'analyse des stéréotypes* of the French from Activity 1. Have students return to the TrackStar lesson and move on to item 4 to discover how much truth, if any, exists in these stereotypes. These articles are reports and informed analyses of French culture, ostensibly written in a way that avoids stereotypes. As the students read these articles, they should fill out Handout 1, *La vérité et les stéréotypes* (Figure 4.9), which asks them to classify stereotypes of France into categories of cultural myth, generalization, and cultural reality. Since students already did this with the American stereotypes in Activity 2, they should be able to work efficiently with only a short review.

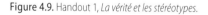

| La vérité et les stéréotypes | | |
|---|---|---|
| **Les mythes culturels** | **Les généralisations** | **Les vérités culturelles** |
| | | |

**Figure 4.9.** Handout 1, *La vérité et les stéréotypes.*

### Expansion

As a follow-up task, engage students in a more involved exercise based on the previous activity and on material to which they have been previously exposed. In small groups, have students complete Handout 2, *Les articles et les stéréotypes*, which will help them gain a deeper understanding of the complexity of stereotypes through the analysis of websites. This will also teach them analysis techniques, which they can take with them into the final project. Collect the handouts at the end of class.

## Extensions

Students with more knowledge of French could conduct an interview in French—either through e-mail, via Skype, or face-to-face via videoconferencing—of a French person (from France or another French-speaking country) about their perceptions of Americans. Questions could range from the concrete (What clothing does a typical American wear?) to the abstract (Why do you think these stereotypes of Americans exist?), depending on the proficiency of the student. The student could also question the French person about some of the stereotypes that Americans have of the French.

Questions about these stereotypes could be included in a final exam or a year-end summative assessment. Students could be given stereotypes of the French and be required to categorize them in French as positive/negative/neutral or products/practices/perspectives. This would verify that they understood the main concepts of the unit.

Students could also conduct surveys about stereotypes of the French with students and adults in the school who do not speak French (you might use an online survey provider such as Survey Monkey or Google Forms). The French students could then prepare presentations of these findings, including graphic representations. Although the survey would have to be in English, the presentation and graphs could be in French, perhaps using PowerPoint or Google Presentations.

## Teaching Tips

More mature students could seek out English sources that address French stereotypes themselves. Articles in English about French news can be found through the search engines at American publication sites, particularly those of local papers and *U.S. News and World Report* (www.usnews.com). Advanced students could read French newspaper articles. See additional sources on the CD.

A note of caution regarding the temporary nature of certain online materials: Accessing news channels is very easy, since most major French news broadcasts are freely accessible through the Internet in a digital format. These are updated daily and are made available shortly after the actual TV broadcast. However, generally speaking, news broadcasts are available only for a limited period of time and are replaced by more recent material on a regular basis. Teachers should take this into account and plan accordingly.

This unit both introduces students to the idea of stereotypes and allows them to discuss cultural stereotypes more openly and with less fear. Once the subject of the long-standing, widely accepted stereotypes that Americans have of the French has been broached, students have license to examine the stereotypes, challenge them, and ultimately see how they function in American ways of viewing the world.

This unit lends itself well to interdisciplinary work, including English, ethics, and history. As they work through the unit, students become more reflective concerning the truth of stereotypes they have about other cultures. Students develop their ability to read current media using critical techniques they have developed in these activities. In turn, students bring their new understanding of stereotypes to other classes, all while learning a lot about the French culture and its realities.

# ASSESSING THE UNIT

## UNIT ASSESSMENT
*Activity 5 (Days 9–14)*

### Preview

Divide students into groups of three or four, or have students select their groups. The final project consists of a 10-minute group oral presentation conducted with the support of multimedia (PowerPoint, Google Presentations, or similar presentation software with a minimum of nine slides, and digital audio and video). Using multimedia technology will give students an opportunity to develop presentational skills for future professional or academic settings. Ask students to be creative in their use of technology and utilize whatever media they see fit (digital sound/videos, graphics, effects, etc.) to support their presentation. The use of multimedia will need to be well thought out and not detract from the content of the project. To ensure that learners develop appropriate presentational skills using these tools, provide guidelines and a formal explanation in class (see Handout 1, *Directions for the Final Project*). Each student should take up a particular responsibility for the final project, which will be part of the student's grade.

The presentation requires students to teach others what they have learned during the course of the unit. Assess students on the content as well as the language. Their presentation will need to follow a particular outline:

**1. Introduction**

- Define stereotypes and the three categories of stereotypes.

**2. First Section**

- Give an example of a cultural myth about the French.

- Give an example of where you have seen this myth in the U.S. (movie, TV, books, etc.).

- Explain the cultural myth's relationship to French culture.

### 3. Second Section

- Give an example of a generalization about the French.

- Give an example of where you have seen this generalization in the U.S. (movie, TV, books, etc.).

- Explain the generalization's relationship to French culture.

### 4. Third Section

- Give an example of a cultural reality about the French.

- Give an example of where you have seen this cultural reality in the U.S. (movie, TV, books, etc.).

- Explain the cultural reality's relationship to French culture.

### 5. Conclusion

- Describe what you have learned about stereotypes through the course of the unit.

- State whether you feel that stereotypes have any importance or value in cultural connections.

See the CD for details concerning what will be discussed in class.

## Assessment Criteria

The final grade of this unit will be based on individual scores for Activities 1, 2, 3, and 4, and on a group score for the final project, Activity 5. Students will also be evaluated on their particular contribution to the final project.

The grade for the final project will cover the following:

- the oral presentation

- the slideshow accompanying the oral presentation

- the written commentary that accompanies each slide, supplying the script, the name of the person responsible for the slide, and the justification for the multimedia elements selected

Rubrics for the assessment tasks in this unit are provided on the CD as well as in Appendix A:

- Rubric for the Final Project—a student-oriented version appears under Activity 5 Handout 2 on the CD and another version appears under Unit 2 Rubrics in Appendix A and on the CD.

- Rubric for NETS•S Assessment—Multimedia Presentation Project

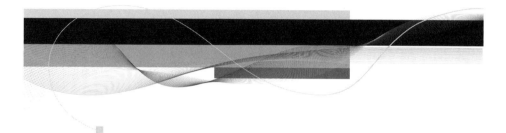

### CHAPTER 5

# Iowa State

## National K–12 Foreign Language Resource Center

## Introduction

*Marcia Harmon Rosenbusch*

The units in this section were created by teachers who attended, or served as leaders for, summer institutes sponsored by the National K–12 Foreign Language Resource Center (NFLRC) at Iowa State University. The NFLRC, which aims to improve student learning of foreign languages at the elementary and secondary school levels, provides professional support for foreign language educators through ongoing research projects, summer institutes, and publications such as the units contained in this section.

Several NFLRC summer institutes have focused on the development of thematic units in the K–12 classroom and others have addressed the use of technology in education. The units in this section are the work of foreign language educators who were part of one or more of these NFLRC summer institutes and represent a rich intertwining of thematic teaching enhanced by technology. While a key component of the institutes is the development of a learning community, and the concept of thematic teaching has been enriched by the work and ideas of all of the institute participants, these units were primarily designed by the following authors: Nancy Gadbois (Unit 3) and Karen Willetts-Kokora (Unit 4).

These units provide examples of thematic teaching that integrate language, culture, and subject content as inspired by Helena Curtain and Carol Ann Dahlberg's seminal work, Languages and Children—Making the Match (Curtain & Dahlberg, 2004). Additionally, the units relate classroom teaching to the national student standards in foreign language education (National Standards, 2006). Both of the units have a cultural focus and exemplify the incorporation of meaningful cultural concepts in classroom teaching. The units address subject content that is developmentally appropriate and provide opportunities for students to enhance their understanding of the second language. Both units utilize similar teaching strategies that include the use of the target language throughout the class by teachers and students, and the use of techniques that appeal to students with diverse learning styles, foster students' ability to think critically and creatively, and facilitate students' ability to work cooperatively in a variety of groupings.

The francophone West Africa unit is designed to enrich the literary and cultural knowledge of the francophone world for upper level secondary students of French; the unit on Carole Fredericks's music, designed for middle and high school students of French, exemplifies cultural assimilation and human achievement. Both of the units can be and have been adapted to other levels of instruction. We hope that these units inspire foreign language teachers to refocus and revitalize their teaching by incorporating technology-rich thematic units into their own K–12 classrooms.

## Resources

Curtain, H. A., & Dahlberg, C. A. (2004). *Languages and children—Making the match* (3rd ed.). Boston, MA: Pearson Education.

National Standards in Foreign Language Education Project. (2006). *Standards for foreign language learning in the 21st century* (3rd ed.). Alexandria, VA: American Council on the Teaching of Foreign Languages (ACTFL).

# Carole Fredericks:
# Music Is Only the Beginning

Carole's story is a wonderful example of cultural assimilation and human achievement. From humble beginnings in Western Massachusetts, Carole evolved into a consummate artist, humanitarian, and citizen of the world.

—Connie Fredericks-Malone

Unit author Nancy Gadbois teaches in the inner-city urban district where Carole Fredericks was born and attended school. Although the school's technology where Nancy teaches will soon be upgraded, she manages with limited access to incorporate multimedia whenever possible. She has described her work on Carole as the highlight of her career. Her students concur.

# OVERVIEW

## AT A GLANCE

**Target Age:** Middle school through post-secondary

**Language:** French

**ACTFL Proficiency Level:** Novice to Intermediate Low

**Primary Content Area:** Foreign Language, Music

**Connections to Other Disciplines:** U.S. and world history, popular culture

**Time Frame:** 1–3 weeks, depending on the depth of the individual project and the intent of the teacher (5 activities, including Unit Assessments)

## UNIT OBJECTIVES

Students will be able to:

- Listen to and interpret several French-language songs and music videos of the late Carole Fredericks.

- Read interviews with and stories about Carole Fredericks in the target language.

- Interview each other on music in general using the target language.

- Use presentation and communications hardware and software to present what they have learned about Carole to others at school and to the community at large.

## DESCRIPTION

In this lesson, students will learn about the life and work of multicultural singer and humanitarian Carole Denise Fredericks of Springfield, Massachusetts. Students will listen to her music, view her music videos, and read authentic press clippings and reviews of the singer in the target language. Carole rose to the top of the music charts in both Europe and West Africa in the 1990s, but until recently was virtually unknown in the United States. She was truly an international musician and star who sang bilingually in French and English and often collaborated with Wolof language artists. During the course of this unit, students will be asked to interpret her music and the stories about her life and work, and present what they have learned to their classmates and the community at large.

This lesson plan can be adapted for use with a variety of age groups, from seventh graders through post-secondary students. Different aspects of the lesson can be shortened or expanded, depending on the age and proficiency level of your students. Ideally, this unit should be taught in a modern language lab with student headsets. However, this unit has been successfully taught in a classroom with only two computers, no lab set-up, and a boom box with no headsets. A classroom equipped with laptop carts will work perfectly for many of the tasks. Activities can also be modified to suit your students' technical facility.

## STANDARDS ADDRESSED

### NETS·S

- Creativity and Innovation 1.a, 1.b
- Communication and Collaboration 2.a, 2.b
- Research and Information Fluency 3.b, 3.c
- Critical Thinking, Problem Solving, and Decision Making 4.b
- Technology Operations and Concepts 6.b

### Standards for Foreign Language Learning

- Communication Standards 1.1, 1.2, 1.3
- Cultures Standard 2.1
- Connections Standards 3.1, 3.2
- Comparisons Standards 4.1, 4.2
- Communities Standards 5.1, 5.2

## CONNECTIONS TO OTHER DISCIPLINES

The musical selections in this unit invoke the United States and world history themes of apartheid, genocide, and equal rights for all. One song discusses the choices that must be made in extreme circumstances, such as in Germany during the Holocaust or South Africa during apartheid. Themes of hunger, children's and women's rights, and the plight of the world's less fortunate populations are also addressed.

This unit also explores the arts, music, and popular culture. The artists' love of their instruments is often highlighted in music videos, as it is in the videos employed in this unit. The interviews and press releases that students will read in this unit discuss musical themes and inspirations and the choices made during the production of songs and videos.

## SPOTLIGHT ON TECHNOLOGY

**Web Browsers.** Students will use the Internet to read and interpret interviews with Carole Fredericks and her fellow musicians in several target-language newspapers. They will also study the official English- and French-language websites dedicated to Carole, and investigate the Wolof language online.

**Word Processing, Presentation, Publishing, and Digital Video-Editing Software.** Students will create reports on the music and life of Carole Fredericks, and use PowerPoint, Google Presentations, Publisher, and/or digital video editing software such as iMovie or Movie Maker to create presentations that they can share with the wider community of learners.

**Asynchronous and Synchronous Communication Software.** Using e-mail, instant messaging, chat, and videoconferencing, students can go beyond the limited communication that occurs within the classroom environment and connect with others to gather information regarding particular topics.

## TECHNOLOGY RESOURCES NEEDED

### Hardware

- computers with Internet access
- CD player
- DVD/VHS player

### Software

- Internet browsing software
- word processing software
- presentation software (e.g., PowerPoint or Google Presentations)
- digital video editing software (e.g., iMovie or Movie Maker)
- publishing software (e.g., Microsoft Publisher)
- asynchronous and synchronous communication software (optional)

## SUPPLEMENTARY RESOURCES

### Web Resources

About.com (review of *Tant qu'elle chante, elle vit!*, a collection of curricular resources built around six of Carole Fredericks's music videos): http://french.about.com/cs/listening/fr/tantquellechant.htm

American Association of Teachers of French (AATF; Carole Fredericks curricular materials): www.frenchteachers.org

Annenberg Media (assessment strategies; teaching foreign languages in K–12; music video online, *A nos actes manqués*): http://learner.org

CaroleFredericks.com (the official French-language site): www.carolefredericks.com

Carole Fredericks fan site: carolefredericksfoundation.org

CDF Music Legacy (the official English-language website dedicated to Carole Fredericks, with numerous learning resources including ordering information for *Tant qu'elle chante, elle vit!*, an integrated package of language-learning activities, worksheets, and a VHS tape or DVD containing six of Carole's music videos including "Un, deux, trois," "Qu'est-ce qui t'amène," and "Respire"): www.cdfmusiclegacy.com

La chaîne de l'espoir (humanitarian organization): www.chainedelespoir.org

Les Enfoirés and the presence of Carole Fredericks: http://ericouaibe.ifrance.com/ericouaibe/enfoires/historique

Lyon People (homage to Carole Fredericks from the city of Lyon): www.lyonpeople.com/news/p1frederiks

MassLive.com (story about Carole Fredericks's family): www.masslive.com (type *Carole Frederick* into the search engine)

NPR: French Lessons Keep Singer's Legacy Alive (National Public Radio story on Carole, with links to audio streams of "Un, deux, trois," "Qu'est-ce qui t'amène," and "Respire" and a video stream of "Un, deux, trois"): www.npr.org/templates/story/story.php?storyId=3857380

Parler d'Sa Vie (interview with Carole Fredericks): www.parler-de-sa-vie.net/ecrits/interviews/19931229.txt

Parler d'Sa Vie (Jean Jacques Goldman/Carole Fredericks interview): www.parler-de-sa-vie.net

Les Restos du Coeur (humanitarian efforts of Carole Fredericks):
www.restosducoeur.org

Tralco-Lingo Fun (where you can purchase the *Couleurs et parfums* CD,
including "Respire," with lesson plans and a "Respire" PDF lesson sample
based on the music video; go to "Teachers" at the top left, and click on
"Carole Fredericks" link on the left menu): www.tralco.com/zeckoShop/US

Wolof Online: www.wolofonline.com

# TEACHING THE UNIT

The following describes 10 days of activities that focus on Carole Fredericks and her
music (many additional learning activities can be found on the CDF Music Legacy
site, www.cdfmusiclegacy.com). Each lesson is identified by title (e.g., Researching
Carole Fredericks) and activity number (e.g., Activity 1).

Because many of the materials for this unit are online, this unit lends itself to being
student-directed.

## RESEARCHING CAROLE FREDERICKS
### *Activity 1 (Days 1–2)*

Students will research online information about Carole Fredericks, both in English
and in French. Depending on the level of detail expected, this work may take two (or
more) days to complete.

### Preview

Prepare an outline of research expectations, including a timeline, to guide the
students and keep them on topic.

### Focused Learning

**Step 1.** Provide students with a list of questions about Carole Fredericks's life and
work to guide their research. The following suggestions are based on the information
available on the French-language website CaroleFredericks.net. These questions are
also provided on the CD as Handout 1.

- D'oú vient Carole?

- Quelle est la date de sa naissance?

- Parlez un peu de sa famille.

- Quelle sorte de musique a-t-elle chantée?

- Elle était membre de quel trio célèbre?

- Oú est-elle décédée, et quand?

- Elle est enterrée dans quel cimetière?

- "Qu'est-ce qui t'amène" a été tourné où aux Etats-Unis?

- Parlez un peu de cette gare.

- Que savez-vous du road-movie "Respire"?

While these questions may seem basic, interpreting them and finding answers on a target-language website can be quite challenging. Adjust the difficulty level of the questions to fit the proficiency level of the class.

**Step 2.** Direct students to explore the two official websites dedicated to Carole Fredericks to learn about her life and music, with the list of research questions as their guide.

- CDF Music Legacy (English): www.cdfmusiclegacy.com

- CaroleFredericks.net (French): www.carolefredericks.net

**Step 3.** After an appropriate amount of time, bring students back to the whole class and discuss what they have discovered about Carole Fredericks's life and music. The format of this discussion and the range of topics covered will depend on the age and proficiency level of the French class. Topics may include the importance of her life, her journey abroad, her impact on the world, and her untimely death in 2001.

## RESEARCHING CAROLE FREDERICKS
*Activity 2 (Day 3)*

Work on the next several days will center on "Un, deux, trois," a song from *Fredericks Goldman Jones*, Carole's 1990 debut album. Free audio and video streams of the song and music video are available on the NPR site (www.npr.org/templates/story/story.php?storyId=3857380), or they can be purchased as part of a larger set of curricular materials and videos titled *Tant qu'elle chante, elle vit!* from the American Association of Teachers of French (AATF) at www.frenchteachers.org. Students will listen to the song, examine the lyrics, and view and interpret the music video.

### Preview

Prepare the song for listening in class. If using the free streaming audio file (best if the classroom has broadband access to the Internet), prepare the computer and speakers and navigate to the NPR site using your web browser. If using the CD, VHS tape, or DVD purchased from AATF, prepare the appropriate playing equipment. Begin the lesson by asking students to speculate what a song called "Un, deux, trois" might be about, basing their answers on what they have learned about Carole Fredericks.

### Focused Learning

**Step 1.** Play the song "Un, deux, trois" to the class.

**Step 2.** Divide the class into pairs and give each pair a copy of the cloze exercise (Handout 1, available on the accompanying CD). The cloze exercise requires students to fill in the blanks to complete the song lyrics.

**Step 3.** Review the answers to the cloze exercise and distribute the song lyrics (Handout 2). Then, have students work in pairs to translate and interpret the song's lyrics. The pairs should look for cognates to help them translate and grasp the meaning of the text.

**Step 4.** When students finish their translations, guide them to the additional online resources listed in the Supplementary Resources section of this lesson, and ask them to find and read articles related to Carole's humanitarian work.

## INTERPRETING THE MUSIC VIDEO FOR "UN, DEUX, TROIS"
*Activity 3 (Day 4)*

Students will present their interpretations of "Un, deux, trois" to the class and arrive at a consensus regarding its major themes. The class will then view the music video for this song and analyze how those themes are portrayed and played out in the video.

### Preview

Prepare the music video for viewing in class. If using the free streaming video file (best if the classroom has broadband access to the Internet), prepare the computer and projection device ahead of time. If using the VHS tape or DVD purchased from AATF, prepare the appropriate playing equipment. Begin the lesson by asking students to speculate on what they might see in the video, based on their knowledge of the song and what they have learned about Carole Fredericks.

### Focused Learning

**Step 1.** Have students share their translations and interpretations of the lyrics to "Un, deux, trois," seeking a consensus on its major themes. Use the questions on the song's lyrics (Handout 1, provided on the CD) to guide this discussion.

**Step 2.** Play the video of "Un, deux, trois" one time through, and have students discuss their initial reactions: What did they see? What did they like? Where was the video filmed? What surprised them about the video or Carole Fredericks's performance?

**Step 3.** Play the video a second time, asking students to pay close attention to the ways that the video depicts, implies, or plays off the major themes that they have identified in the song's lyrics.

**Step 4.** Complete the analysis of the music video with a whole-class discussion.

**Step 5.** Introduce the group presentation assignment that students will be working on over the next several days. Break the students into pairs (or larger groups, if necessary) and have them select a format for their presentation, such as a slideshow (using presentation software), a video (using digital video editing software), or a publication (using a publishing program).

## CREATING THE GROUP PRESENTATIONS
*Activity 4 (Days 5–8)*

Students will work in pairs (or larger groups) to create a project that introduces Carole Fredericks to another group of students studying French in their own or a different school, or to their parents, or to the community at large.

### Preview

Review the discussions of the past two days and give students a copy of the rubrics that will be used to assess their performance on the group presentation project. (The student-oriented versions of the three rubrics are contained in Activity 4 Handout 1 on the CD.)

### Focused Learning

**Step 1.** Have students analyze the rubrics for both the oral presentation and technology tasks and make sure they understand what is expected of them as they complete their projects.

**Step 2.** Direct students to begin designing storyboard outlines or layouts for their project. Also, have them brush up on the technical skills needed to complete their particular project: a slideshow, a video, or a publication. Completing this project may take several days, depending on the technical facility of the students and the amount of class time they can devote to this project.

**Step 3.** As students work on their presentations over the next several days, encourage them to review the rubrics periodically, refine their outlines, and invite peer evaluations of their work-in-progress.

## DELIVERING THE GROUP PRESENTATIONS
*Activity 5 (Days 9–10)*

### Preview

Prepare the classroom for the group presentations.

### Focused Learning

**Step 1.** Have each pair or group share their presentation with the class.

**Step 2.** After each presentation, ask students to peer-evaluate the projects anonymously, based on the rubrics given to the whole class.

**Step 3.** Collect these evaluations at the end of each class period (if presentations extend over more than one day).

## UNIT EXTENSION AND TEACHING TIPS

### Unit Extension Activities

Students can be asked to present their work to another French class at school, or to nearby elementary or middle school French students. Student presentations can also be video recorded for sharing beyond the school setting.

Students may also contact (by e-mail) members of the Fredericks family, including sister Connie Fredericks-Malone, at www.cdfmusiclegacy.com.

Although this unit is dedicated to Carole Fredericks, any popular musical icon who would interest today's students could be studied in a similar manner.

### Unit Teaching Tips

Before you start, clearly identify your desired outcomes and consider alternative assessment strategies that will better engage your learners. To help you with this process, visit http://learner.org/resources/series185.html where you can view a digital video that covers three different types of foreign language assessment. Scroll down the article "Teaching Foreign Languages K–12: A Library of Classroom Practices" until you see "3. Assessment Strategies." Select the video-on-demand link at the right. All worksheets created for this project are downloadable. The site is free of charge, but will require you to supply some basic information to access resources. The video describes assessment strategies for all three communicative modes: Interpretive, Interpersonal, and Presentational.

Because students are generally enthusiastic about any technology, and also love music, this project is almost guaranteed to be of high interest. This unit has been used in large classes that have included learners of all styles as well as gifted and special needs students. Although logistics and limited technology access can occasionally be a hindrance, you would never know this by the excitement generated when the mobile cart is wheeled into the classroom.

Be aware that some students may need help when using technology to create their projects. Many students, even those who may also be enrolled in technology classes, may have no idea how to perform foreign language-specific tasks such as inserting accents or using online translation services. Never assume anything!

# ASSESSING THE UNIT

## UNIT ASSESSMENT

Several forms of evaluation may be used to assess student performance. These may include the following:

**Activity 1.** Teachers can create a "treasure hunt" worksheet based on the two official websites, and use these for formative assessment.

**Activities 2 and 3.** The students' translations and responses to the interpretive questions about the meaning of the lyrics to "Un, deux, trois" can be used for assessment purposes. Teachers can also assess student comprehension of the online articles they read during these activities.

**Activity 4.** Formative evaluation of the group presentations-in-progress should be based on the three rubrics handed out to students. Frequent feedback should be provided to students while they are working on their projects to help them improve their final presentations.

**Activity 5.** The culminating activity may include both student and teacher evaluations of the final presentation.

### Assessment Criteria

Rubrics for the assessment tasks in this unit are provided in Appendix A as well as on the CD. Units 3 and 4 share the same assessment rubrics: Rubric for Oral Presentation, Rubric for Assessment of National Foreign Language Standards, and Rubric for Assessment of NETS•S.

# UNIT 4

# The Culture and Literature of Francophone West Africa

Un veillard qui meurt, c'est une bibliothèque qui brûle.
*(For each elder who dies, a library burns.)*

—Amadou Hampaté Bâ

This unit was developed by Karen Willetts-Kokora, an author for *Foreign Language Instructional Guides for Upper Levels of French* for the Montgomery County Public Schools (MCPS). It is part of the French 5 theme Discovery and History. The MCPS secondary curriculum for Upper Levels 4–6 is content-based foreign language instruction within thematic units. This unit is an expansion of the original material and has been written with a focus on technology integration. The lessons now include several opportunities to participate in technology-enhanced tasks to assist teachers in integrating various technology tools seamlessly into their instruction. The activities teachers choose to implement in class may depend upon which technology resources are available in their school.

# OVERVIEW

## AT A GLANCE

**Target Age:** High school, Grades 9–12

**Language:** French

**ACTFL Proficiency Level:** Intermediate Mid to Intermediate High

**Primary Content Area:** Cultural studies

**Connections to Other Disciplines:** Geography, history, music, folklore, literature

**Time Frame:** 4 weeks

## UNIT OBJECTIVES

Students will be able to:

- Identify West-African francophone countries and capitals on a map.

- Present information about the geography, history, government, economics (including products), and languages of a selected francophone West African country.

- Explain the CFA monetary system (le franc de la Communauté Financière Africaine) and discuss important cultural symbols and information depicted on CFA bills (including art, animals, clothing, lifestyles, plants, and other cultural objects).

- Compare CFA money with the Euro from a cultural and historical point of view.

- Describe major West African instruments and state how music is integral to the African oral tradition.

- Read and understand sample folktales from francophone West Africa (with a focus on Bernard Dadié from Côte d'Ivoire).

- Investigate the use of African languages in traditional folktales and the role of the *griot*, or storyteller.

- Examine connections to European folktales and discuss how messages or morals in the stories reflect various traditional cultural values.

### Language Objectives

Students will be able to:

- Practice the use of prepositions with geographical terms, countries, and capitals.

- Correctly identify and write past tenses of a variety of verbs (*passé composé, imparfait, passé simple*).

- Develop a repertoire of African-specific French vocabulary.

- Increase use of a variety of transition words, adverbs of time, and expressions included in traditional tales.

- Write an original folktale using vocabulary, structures, and other features typical of this genre.

### Technology Objectives

Students will be able to:

- Conduct Internet research using authentic French language websites.

- Use software to organize, classify, and present findings.

- Collaborate electronically with other students and with the teacher.

- Use software to develop a presentation or a website to share their projects with the class.

## STANDARDS ADDRESSED

### NETS•S

- Creativity and Innovation 1.a, 1.b

- Communication and Collaboration 2.a, 2.b, 2.c

- Research and Information Fluency 3.b, 3.c

- Critical Thinking, Problem Solving, and Decision Making 4.b, 4.c

- Technology Operations and Concepts 6.b

### Standards for Foreign Language Learning

- Communication Standards 1.1, 1.2, 1.3

- Cultures Standards 2.1, 2.2

- Connections Standards 3.1, 3.2

- Comparisons Standards 4.1, 4.2

- Communities Standard 5.1

## DESCRIPTION

This unit touches on a variety of aspects of francophone West Africa and is written for upper-level secondary students of French (whose proficiency is Intermediate Mid to Intermediate High) to enrich their literary and cultural knowledge of the francophone world outside of Europe. Textbooks in French are often very Eurocentric; thus, this unit could supplement a variety of high-school French courses. Lessons include basic geography, history, and country profiles. Information on the West African monetary system, oral tradition, musical instruments, and typical African poems and folktales is provided. The unit time frame is approximately four weeks, but teachers may select smaller portions of activities or expand the lessons to meet their own objectives.

The unit begins with a review of the geography of francophone West Africa. A country profile of Côte d'Ivoire or Sénégal is presented, with students then asked to investigate another county's geography, history, government, economy, ethnic groups, and languages. Students will conduct Internet research and present their findings orally to the class. They may also use presentation software, publishing software, or a website development program at the teacher's discretion.

The next activities provide an overview of the CFA franc and the monetary system. Students are asked to visually analyze CFA currency and consider the cultural aspects of the animals, plants, peoples, and typical African objects and art printed on the money. A comparison can then be made with the Euro and the cultural information represented on these bills. Again, research will be conducted online. Students may use concept mapping software (e.g., Inspiration) to organize their findings. Students may also use electronic communication tools (e.g., e-mail, chat, Skype) to collaborate and interact with peers and the teacher about their findings or to report results.

Poems and two traditional folktales by Bernard Dadié of Côte d'Ivoire follow a section on the role of the *griot,* or storyteller, and musical instruments in African oral tradition. One of the tales includes examples of Baoulé, an Ivoirian language and an important ethnic group. Teachers may wish to expand this example to other African languages, especially if Haitian or African students are in their class. Websites of various African instruments, music, artists, and languages can also be explored.

Students are then asked to compare African and European folktales to investigate cultural differences. Numerous websites of traditional African and European tales are available, some with sound recordings of the tales in French (see Supplementary Resources and Resources for Activities, pages 111–115).

The last section provides students with an opportunity to write their own folktale and thus demonstrate the language skills and cultural knowledge acquired in this unit. As a culminating project or summative assessment, students can videotape or make a podcast of their original tale. If digital video cameras are available, students may incorporate original video clips into their presentations. They may also choose to publish a collection of the classes' tales using a word processor or publishing tool. Students could also present their original stories (or dialogues made from them) to other French classes, at a French club meeting, or at a cultural event at the school or in the community.

The complete unit, including lesson plans, student handouts, visual aids, teacher keys, and assessment ideas, is included on the accompanying CD.

## CONNECTIONS TO OTHER DISCIPLINES

Students will study geography and history through their exposure to francophone areas outside of continental Europe and will have the opportunity to study one or more of these regions in more depth. Teachers can expand the content provided in this unit to include a discussion of the role of France and other colonizing countries in the history and current day-to-day life of francophone Africa.

An exploration of *literature* and *oral tradition* is naturally suited to the topic of francophone West Africa. While oral tradition in Africa is and was carried out in numerous local African languages, students will have the occasion to read poems and folktales translated by African authors into the French language. The griot, or storyteller, is essential to oral tradition and the recognition of African life events, such as rites of passage and funerals. Teachers may expand these lessons to include chapters from recommended AP French literature books, such as *L'Enfant noir* (Camara Laye) and *Une si longue lettre* (Miriama Bâ).

Music is an integral part of oral tradition and contemporary life in franco-phone Africa. In this unit, students are given the opportunity to advance their understanding of *music,* as well as *ethnomusicology* and *African languages.* One lesson provides background information on typical African instruments. Students could expand their knowledge and interests by exploring traditional musicians such as Lamine Konté and Daili Djimo Kouyate or more contemporary African singers such as Youssou N'Dour and MC Solaar. Many of the artists sing in local African languages, as well as in French. Students could preview some lyrics provided on websites to explore how African languages are written. A study of the musical systems and "drum language" is also possible if the teacher has local colleagues or specialists to assist in developing an interdisciplinary lesson.

## SPOTLIGHT ON TECHNOLOGY

**Web Browsers.** While many resources are provided within the unit, students will need to find additional information on the Internet to expand their knowledge base and their language learning. Using authentic websites in French will help students develop reading and comprehension skills. In this unit, students will conduct Internet research to obtain historical and cultural information.

**Projection System.** The teacher can use a projection system or interactive white board to share aspects of the lesson with the class and to project a shared wiki.

**Database and Encyclopedia Software.** Numerous informational databases and multimedia encyclopedias are available (although some are online and may require a subscription through a school's media center). Popular resources include *Gale Student Resource Center* (culture and country information), *SIRS Researcher, ProQuest* (foreign language newspapers and magazines), *Wikipedia,* and *Britannica Online School Edition.* Students should learn to select and evaluate various information resources, not just Internet resources, as part of a media literacy unit.

**Synchronous and Asynchronous Communication Software.** Students can enhance their receptive and productive language skills by using e-mail, chats, instant messaging, Skype, and other communication technologies to exchange information, comments, opinions, or analyses of various topics under study in this unit. Discussions may take place on a virtual discussion medium available on a school's local area network (LAN). For example, students may conduct peer-review feedback on draft assignments by posting to a virtual discussion board such as Blackboard. Student may also use Yahoo! Groups for communal e-mails for group projects. Keep in mind, however, that e-mails, chats, and instant messaging may be difficult for teachers to monitor.

**Blogs.** Students may contribute to blogs, or online journals, to exchange information, even with French students abroad (several popular websites are posted for French-speaking "bloggers"). Communication with native speakers of the language will enhance students' language skills, although, again, it may be difficult for teachers to control or monitor blogs.

It is interesting to note that a *paralanguage* or *Internet language* has developed in both French and English, changing many words and spellings in electronic communications. Students enjoy exploring and using these new terms in activities.

**Word Processing Software.** Student assignments, assessments, and creative projects may require the production of various authentic text types (e.g., essays, letters, or personal journal entries). In addition, tables, graphs, and charts will enhance the organization and logical presentation of word processed documents. Word processing programs also provide the possibility of easily transposing documents into HTML format for websites. Google Docs allows students on multiple computers at different locations to all collaborate on a single document simultaneously.

**Presentation Software, Publishing Programs, and Multimedia Authoring Tools.** Student projects and presentations (such as class newsletters, journals, or brochures) can be enhanced by the use of programs such as Microsoft Publisher, PowerPoint, Google Presentations, HyperStudio, or more powerful multimedia authoring tools. These multimedia programs allow students to be more creative with graphics, sounds, music, and video clips incorporated into their presentations. Many of these authoring programs also provide a way to save projects as HTML documents to import into websites. If students have access to a digital camera with video/still capabilities, they may capture images and edit them into their presentations, or consider having them remix existing digital video clips. Multimedia software includes: (for Mac) iMovie, FinalCut Pro; (for PC) AVID, Adobe Premiere, Windows Movie Maker.

**Concept Mapping Software.** Concept mapping software such as Inspiration can expand learners' ability to conceptualize and organize their knowledge, and can help them outline and plan more complex oral and written projects—an important academic skill for all content areas. Because this software requires learners to visually map their thinking processes, it can also help support different intelligences and learning styles.

**Online Maps.** Online mapping websites such as Google Earth, Google Maps, and Mapquest are a great resource for students. They allow you to zoom in and out and calculate distances and routes.

**Graphics Software.** Graphics software such as a drawing or painting program can be used to illustrate ideas. These tools appeal to visual learners.

**Web Publishing Software or Web Editors.** Students who are more advanced technology users may produce their projects on a website. Many free HTML editors, web editors, and site builders are widely accessible. For free programs, teachers may consult: www. thefreecountry.com/sitemap.shtml. Google Sites allows easy publishing to the web without the necessity of knowing HTML or other code.

Students who are experienced in JavaScript may enhance their websites by improving layout of the web pages or the navigation of the site and by adding special graphical effects or dynamic web page content.

**Wikis.** Wikis serve as a resource repository and reference on a particular topic and are particularly suited to group work and collaboration. Wikis can store vocabulary words, timelines, lists of facts, and examples of student work, and they allow the students themselves to do the creation, editing, and maintenance.

## TECHNOLOGY RESOURCES NEEDED

### Hardware

- computers with Internet access
- projection system or interactive white board
- CD-audio player (for musical selections not on the Internet)
- digital video/still camera (optional)
- voice recording equipment (optional)

### Software

- Internet browsing software
- databases and encyclopedias (some may be accessed online)
- access to a class blog (optional)
- synchronous and asynchronous communication software (e-mail, IM, chat, Skype)
- word processing software
- presentation software, publishing programs, and multimedia authoring tools
- concept mapping software (e.g., Inspiration)

- online mapping software

- graphics software

- access to a wiki (optional)

- web publishing software or web editors (optional)

## SUPPLEMENTARY RESOURCES

### Online Dictionaries

ARTFL Project: French-English Dictionary Form:
http://artfl-project.uchicago.edu

French Dictionary Online: www.online-dictionary.net/french/index.htm

### Technology Publications Online

Learning & Leading with Technology: www.iste.org/ll

THE Journal: Technological Horizons in Education: www.thejournal.com

Technology and Learning: www.techlearning.com

### Cultural Resources on Francophone Africa

Montgomery County Public Schools. (1994). *Teaching culture in Grades K–8:
A resource manual for teachers of French*. Rockville, MD: Author.

Montgomery County Public Schools. (1998). *Les cultures des pays francophones de
l'Afrique de l'Ouest: A resource manual and CD-ROM (Mac only) for teachers of
French*. Rockville, MD: Author.

*Note: The illustrations and maps used in Unit 4 activities are from the aforemen-
tioned MCPS publications. They are used by permission.*

### The Technology Gap in the Developing World

Coste, P. (2000, 27 avril–3 mai). Tous égaux face au Web? *L'Express*, 2547.
www.lexpress.fr/informations/tous-egaux-face-au-web_637660.html

## RESOURCES FOR ACTIVITIES 1–2 (DAYS 1–4)

### Background Information on the Francophone World

Valette, J.-P. (2000). *Discovering French—Rouge: Level 3*. Chicago, IL:
McDougal Littell/Houghton Mifflin.

### Maps

Map Resources: www.mapresources.com

WorldAtlas.Com: http://worldatlas.com/webimage/testmaps/maps.htm

### Nation Profiles

Abidjan.net: www.abidjan.net

BBC NEWS: Country Profiles:
http://news.bbc.co.uk/2/hi/country_profiles/default.stm

iSenegal: http://isenegal.free.fr/senegal

Library of Congress, Country Studies: Côte d'Ivoire:
http://lcweb2.loc.gov/frd/cs/citoc.html

Le Senegal Online: http://senegal-online.com/index

### History and Geography

Grove, A. T. (1989). *The changing geography of Africa*. Oxford, England: Oxford University Press. Information and maps of Africa from various time periods.

## RESOURCES FOR ACTIVITIES 3–4 (DAYS 5–7)

Banque des Etats de l'Afrique Centrale (BEAC): www.beac.int

European Central Bank (Euro Banknotes): www.ecb.europa.eu/euro/banknotes

Valette, J.-P., & Valette, R. M. (2001). *Discovering French: Europak copymasters*. Chicago: McDougal Littell. Includes explanation of designs on Euros, maps, and many activities.

## RESOURCES FOR ACTIVITIES 5–9 (DAYS 8–14)

### Oral Tradition

Gambian Griot: School of Music and Dance:
http://home.planet.nl/~verka067/Links.html

Griot: www.griot.de

### African Musical Instruments

Les arts africains: www.musee-manega.bf/fr/arts/artsafricains/artsaf.htm

Guide to the Ethnomusicology LP Collection in the Oberlin College
Conservatory Library:
www.oberlin.edu/faculty/rknight/LPcollection/Lists/5c.westafrica.html

Instruments de musique Africains (sanza, kora, balafon):
www.decorationafricaine.com/instrument-de-musique-Instrument-de-
Musique-Africain-ccnaaaaaa.asp

Les instruments de musique en Afrique de l'Ouest:
www.artisanat-africain.com/instruments/les_instruments_de_musique

Kora-music.com (MP3 sound samples and software downloads):
www.kora-music.com

Metronimo.com (quiz: les instruments de musique africains):
www.metronimo.com/fr/jeux/quiz/quiz64.php

La musique au Sénégal: www.senegalaisement.com/senegal/musique

## African Music Websites

African Music and Drumming Resources on the Web:
http://echarry.web.wesleyan.edu/africother.html

Afropop Worldwide: www.afropop.org

African Music Home Page: http://biochem.chem.nagoya-u.ac.jp/~endo/africa

Frank Bessem's Musiques d'Afrique: http://musiques-afrique.com

## Text Sources for La Légende baoulé

Herbst, H. L., & Sturges, H. (1996). *Par tout le monde francophone: Cours
intermédiaire*. New York, NY: Longman.

Valette, J.-P. (2000). *Discovering French—Rouge: Level 3*. Chicago, IL:
McDougal Littell/Houghton Mifflin.

## Audio Source for La Légende baoulé

Konté, L. (1989). *La kora du Sénégal* (Vol. 2) [CD]. Paris, France: Arion.

## Children's Literature and Folktales (Contes)

ContesAfricains.com: Le site des contes et de la littérature orale (African
folktales): www.contesafricains.com

Ocelot, M. (2001). *Kirikou et la sorcière*. Paris, France: Milan.

Ocelot, M., & Andrieu, P. (2002). *Kirikou et la hyène noire*. Paris, France: Milan.

Ocelot, M., & Andrieu, P. (2003). *Kirikou et le buffle aux cornes d'or*. Paris, France: Milan.

Vary, A., & Brouillet, C. (1997). *Contes et légendes du monde francophone: A collection of tales from the French-speaking world*. Chicago, IL: National Textbook Company.

Vary, A., & Brouillet, C. (2004). *Contes et fables d'Afrique*. Columbus, OH: Glencoe/McGraw-Hill.

### Grammar Practice

Quia: www.quia.com

### Le Pagne noir

Dadié, B. B. (1955). *Le Pagne noir*. Paris, France: Présence Africaine. (Out of print.)

### Kirikou et la sorcière

Ocelot, M. (Director and writer). (1998). *Kirikou et la sorcière*. [74-minute animated film for children, in French with English subtitles. Original sound track by Senegal's Youssou N'Dour]. (Available from ArtMattan Productions, New York, NY; www.kirikou.net; e-mail: ArtMattan@AfricanFilm.com. Also available with 54-page French activity guide [2003] from FilmArobics, www.filmarobics.com; e-mail: film@filmarobics.com.)

### Cinderella (Cendrillon)

Cendrillon de Charles Perrault (Perrault version of Cendrillon): www.alalettre.com/perrault-cendrillon.htm

Les contes de Grimm (Grimm version of Cendrillon): www.chez.com/feeclochette/grimm.htm

Histoire Cendrillon: www.coindespetits.com/histoires/histcendrillon/cendrillon

## RESOURCES FOR ACTIVITY 10 (DAYS 15–18)

### African Authors

#### Miriama Bâ
Afrik.com: www.afrik.com/article3517.html

Lire les femmes écrivains et les littératures africaines:
www.arts.uwa.edu.au/AFLIT/BaMariama.html

Literary Encyclopedia: www.litencyc.com/php/speople.php?rec=true&UID=5152

**Fatou Ndiaye Sow**

Lire les femmes écrivains et les littératures africaines:
www.arts.uwa.edu.au/AFLIT/NdiayeSowFatou.html

**Bernard Dadié**

Dadié, B. B. (1955). *Le pagne noir*. Paris, France: Présence Africaine. (Out of print.)

**Camara Laye**

Résumé de *L'Enfant noir* (AP exam preparation document):
www.sonoma.edu/users/t/toczyski/camaralaye/clayeresume

Les Films du Paradoxe (information on the 1995 film *L'Enfant noir* by Laurent Chevallier based on the Camara Laye novel):
www.filmsduparadoxe.com/enfantcat

**Léopold Sédar Senghor**

Académie française: www.academie-francaise.fr/immortels/base/academiciens/fiche.asp?param=666

iSenegal: Léopold Sédar Senghor: http://isenegal.free.fr/senghor.htm

Senghor au club des poètes: www.franceweb.fr/poesie/senghor2.htm

## African Proverbs

Reseau Ivoire: www.rezoivoire.net/Litteratures

# TEACHING THE UNIT

The following discussion summarizes 10 activities that focus on the culture and literature of francophone West Africa. Each lesson is identified by title (e.g., Money and Culture) and activity number (e.g., Activity 4). Complete activities, including lesson plans, visual aids, student handouts, teacher keys, and assessment ideas, are included on the accompanying CD. Content, language, and technology objectives are listed for each block of activities.

## OBJECTIVES FOR ACTIVITIES 1–2
*(Days 1–4)*

### Content

Students will be able to:

- Name the countries and capitals of francophone Africa.
- Describe an African francophone country in more detail.

### Language

Students will be able to:

- Use prepositions correctly with countries, cities, and geographical places.
- Describe basic features of a country using appropriate vocabulary and structures.

### Technology

Students will be able to:

- Use technology research tools (such as the Internet).
- Use technology communication tools (such as e-mail).
- Use technology productivity tools (such as word processing software, PowerPoint, or Publisher).

## GEOGRAPHY OF FRANCOPHONE WEST AFRICA
*Activity 1 (Day 1)*

### Preview

Review with students their previous knowledge of the geography of francophone West Africa and the use of prepositions with countries and cities. Remind students that they will mainly be looking for the names of francophone (rather than Anglophone or lusophone) countries, although the other countries' official languages may be discussed later. These countries should have been studied before in lower levels of French, so this is considered a review.

### Focused Learning

Display Transparency 1a, a map of Africa without the names of countries. In small groups, have students write the names of the countries they know on a blank map (Handout 1a). Encourage groups to consult with one another until most countries have been identified. Then, in a whole class follow-up, display Transparency 1b with the names of each country so that students can verify their responses.

Review the names of countries and their capitals as necessary, using a large map of Africa. Then, review prepositions with countries and cities as needed. Have students complete tasks in which they identify the correct prepositions and then match West African countries with their capitals (Handout 2a). Finally, assess student knowledge of the capitals of these countries (Handout 2b).

### Expansion

As an expansion activity, students can review French vocabulary for geographical features, such as deserts, mountains, and rivers (Google Earth is a wonderful resource). As an additional expansion activity, students may explore new content regarding how West Africa was divided by the colonial powers into arbitrary divisions that did not reflect existing ethnic groups and historical kingdoms. This could be an interdisciplinary activity with a social studies or world history teacher. A wiki can be a great repository for research done by students as well as new vocabulary terms.

As a technology extension, students can be asked to find various online maps—topographical, political, population density, and so on—to provide them with more information about the region they will be studying in-depth during their individual (or small group) projects about selected African countries in Activity 2.

### Teaching Tips

If African students are present in the classroom (or in the school), they can serve as experts in the small group activities or in the upcoming projects on francophone Africa.

## COUNTRY PROFILES: CÔTE D'IVOIRE AND SÉNÉGAL
*Activity 2 (Days 2–4)*

### Preview

Begin with a whole-group focus on one of the more well-known francophone countries—Côte d'Ivoire or Sénégal (usually included briefly in most French textbooks). Have students mention a few facts they know about Côte d'Ivoire or Sénégal.

As a preassessment, have pairs or small groups of students fill in any background knowledge they possess about these countries on a country profile chart (Handout 1; Figure 5.1). You may want to assign topics to the groups, based on the chart categories.

## Que savez-vous déjà au sujet de la Côte d'Ivoire ou du Sénégal ?

| Géographie : Villes, Fleuves | Histoire : Indépendance | Gouvernement et Président | Economie et Produits Agricoles | Langues et Groupes Ethniques |
|---|---|---|---|---|
| Côte d'Ivoire | | | | |
| Sénégal | | | | |

Pour les renseignements sur le Sénégal, visitez le site de la « Toile » suivante : www.senegal-online.com/index.html

Figure 5.1. Excerpt from Activity 2 Handout 1.

## Focused Learning

Have groups of students report back to the class, who will take notes on the information provided. Using web resources on Sénégal and the Background Information Sheets for Côte d'Ivoire provided on the CD, help students complete various details missing in the chart. These teacher pages can also be used as a "model report" (or anchor paper) for students. Using Handout 2 as a guide, have students practice writing paragraphs from their notes on a word processor. The result will be a short report on Côte d'Ivoire or Sénégal that serves as a model for a future research project.

## Expansion

Have individual students or groups select another francophone African country they wish to investigate in more detail to create a country profile report. Topics explored may include geography, history, government, economics, ethnic groups, languages, and famous people, such as leaders and authors. Have student groups conduct research in the computer lab or media center to complete their reports. They may wish to consult database or encyclopedia software as research tools. If students work in groups, they should use e-mail or some other type of electronic communication to collaborate and interact with each other during the research and peer-editing processes.

Have students make presentations to other class members when the reports are completed. As oral presentations are given, students may take notes on additional copies of Handout 1 or Handout 2.

As a technology alternative, students or groups could also produce a mini-project using a presentation program such as PowerPoint, create a "country profile" brochure using software such as Publisher, or develop a web page.

### Teaching Tips

It could take several days in the computer lab for students to complete this research project, depending upon the required length and the technology used. If all students have access to computers at home, much of the assignment could be conducted outside of class time, which would encourage collaborative electronic communication among students. Google Docs allows multiple students at separate locations to collaborate on a single document simultaneously.

## OBJECTIVES FOR ACTIVITIES 3–4
*(Days 5–7)*

### Content

Students will be able to:

- Explain the basics of the monetary system used in francophone Africa.

### Language

Students will be able to:

- Expand the vocabulary needed to discuss cultural elements.

- Describe symbols found on money, including art objects, plants, people, and clothing.

- Compare and contrast cultural similarities and differences.

## Technology

Students will be able to:

- Use technology research tools (such as the Internet).

- Use technology communication tools (such as e-mail).

- Use technology productivity tools (concept mapping software such as Inspiration, word processing software).

# CFA FRANCS
*Activity 3 (Days 5–6)*

Students will study the monetary system used in the francophone African countries and examine several CFA francs (monetary units). They will discuss the various representations depicted on this currency and how these items reflect local cultures. Images of several denominations of CFA francs are provided on the CD and more can be found on the website listed for the Banque des Etats de l'Afrique Centrale (BEAC), www.beac.int.

## Preview

Read the Background Information Sheet on CFA Francs (included on the CD) aloud with students or distribute it to students as Handout 1 and have them read it at home. Go over the basic questions about CFA at the end of the article. Show pictures of the bills (Transparency 1), and introduce how CFA francs reflect the cultures of West Africa. Use the questions after the pictures of each bill to point out various items. Encourage students to answer these questions aloud during the class discussion. You may wish to show additional bills by accessing the BEAC website. You may also wish to distribute paper copies of the overheads to students (Handout 2).

## Focused Learning

Brainstorm with a word splash or other activity to help students create an appropriate vocabulary list to assist them in filling out the cultural chart (Handout 3). The exercise asks students to identify clothing styles, animals, plants, and other cultural objects depicted on various bills. Students may need a specific list of African cultural terms (see CD: Teacher Key for Handouts 3 and 4).

Discuss the cultural representations that can be found on the money bills. For example, ask students: What is depicted to represent the local lifestyle, geographic area, clothing, animals, and languages? Then have students complete Handout 3 in pairs, and afterwards, compare answers in small or large groups (Figure 5.2).

## Fiche d'étudiant 3 : CFA Francs : Intro-vocabulaire

*Examiner les billets CFA. Avec un/une collègue, faites une liste des éléments culturels qui y sont représentés. Pensez au mode de vie, à la région géographique, aux vêtements, aux animaux, aux plantes, à la langue utilisée… Partagez les idées avec un autre groupe.*

| Modes de vie | Région(s) géographique(s) | Style de vêtements |
|---|---|---|
| Animaux | Plantes-produits agricoles | Autres objets culturels |

**Figure 5.2.** Excerpt from Activity 3 Handout 3.

### Expansion

Have students draw on the previous class discussions and the completed Handout 3 to individually complete a series of questions regarding their cultural study of CFA (Handout 4). Afterward, have them discuss their answers in small groups. As an alternative, you may wish to use Handout 4 as an assessment of students' reading comprehension or as a homework assignment. (Possible answers are listed on the CD, Teacher Key for Handouts 3 and 4.)

For technology-enhanced activities, students can research the web for information about the Zone Franc and obtain pictures of numerous bills dating back to 1919. The BCEA website (listed in Supplementary Resources) has a wealth of information about the choice for designs (motifs) on bills and the history of the CFA franc. Students could also investigate how the bills from one or more countries have changed over time.

### Teaching Tips

Have native francophone speakers research the background of various CFA in different West African countries or other francophone areas (Canada, Belgium, Haiti) and report back to the class. Perhaps they could find sample bills from their country of origin to discuss with the class.

## MONEY AND CULTURE
*Activity 4 (Day 7)*

### Preview

Introduce students to Euro bills. Images of Euro bills are included on the CD and can also be found at the website of the European Central Bank (www.euro.ecb.int/en/section/testnotes.nd5.html). You may also wish to distribute paper copies of the overheads to students (Handout 1).

### Focused Learning

Have students compare CFA bills with Euro currency and discuss what these differences indicate about Europe and West Africa. What are the major differences in money bills from these regions? What do these differences indicate culturally (and historically) about these countries? Discuss as a class or in small groups.

The next task is a formative assessment. Distribute Handout 2, which asks students to pretend they are journalists writing about cultural and historical images found on currency. They are to write an article about the cultural values portrayed on currency from francophone African countries and European countries. They should explain the following: What does a country's money imply about its cultural values? Is currency a kind of official image of a region or nation?

Set guidelines for the expected length of the paper, provide a rubric of criteria, and establish when first and final drafts are due. Have students begin to plan their written answer in class (using Inspiration or a different prewriting tool) so they can ask questions. Instruct them to complete their writing at home on a word processor, if available, and turn in rough drafts for peer and teacher feedback. Drafts may be submitted by e-mail, if desired.

### Create a Class Blog

A classroom blog is a great way to share student writing and give students immediate and varied feedback from their peers.

## Expansion

Students could examine and compare other francophone countries' currency, such as Canada or Haiti. In addition, students could examine U.S. dollar bills and reflect on American culture as portrayed by the symbols, images, and words on currency. Different groups of students could focus on just one other monetary unit and culture and compare them to the CFA francs and West African culture. Groups could then report back orally, which could be followed by a whole-class discussion.

## Teaching Tips

Depending on the level of the class, a more in-depth discussion about symbols in general and cultural symbols in particular may be required before students begin to write. The writing prompt can also be varied according to different students' needs.

# OBJECTIVES FOR ACTIVITIES 5–9
*(Days 8–14)*

## Content

Students will be able to:

- Name and describe typical African musical instruments.

- Explain the storyteller (*griot*) role in African oral tradition.

- State the major components of folktales.

## Language

Students will be able to:

- Expand African vocabulary in French to meet content objectives.

- Compare and contrast cultural values and morals found in European and African folktales (contes).

## Technology

Students will be able to:

- Use technology research tools.

- Use technology communication tools.

- Use technology productivity tools.

## AFRICAN ORAL TRADITION
*Activity 5 (Day 8)*

### Preview

Introduce oral tradition storytelling, the role of the griot, and musical instruments in African cultures. Show pictures of traditional African musical instruments from the Internet. Distribute Handout 1 and have students read about the African oral tradition and discuss the poem "Le tam-tam," by Fatou Ndiaye Sow. Discuss how poetry and music is linked in these cultures.

### Focused Learning

Distribute Handout 2 (Figure 5.3) and have students access the Internet to find pictures and information about traditional African instruments, such as the kora, balafon, riti, or tambour, or instruct them to research a modern-day griot such as Mory Kanté. Students may complete their web search while listening to African music on the web or on CDs, if available. (See Supplementary Resources for African music websites.)

---

### Fiche d'exploration : Les instruments de musique africains et le griot

*Surfez les sites Web suivants et donnez une description de chaque instrument de musique.*

1.  le griot—Quel est son rôle dans la société africaine ?
    www.mali-music.com/cat/catg/griot.htm

2.  la kora (cora)—Comment cet instrument est-il employé dans la musique moderne ?
    www.mali-music.com/cat/instruments/instk/kora.htm

Nommez d'autres instruments que vous avez trouvés sur Internet :

_____

e.g., www.au-senegal.com/art/musique.htm.

Trouvez un site Web avec la musique africaine traditionnelle et/ou moderne et écoutez les chansons. Mettez l'adresse du site ici et partagez-la avec un(e) camarade de classe :

www. _____

---

Figure 5.3. Students conduct Internet research to complete Handout 2.

### Expansion

Distribute Handout 3 (or direct students to http://yclady.free.fr/village3) and have students read and discuss another poem, called "Tam-Tam," by the famous author and former president of Sénégal, Léopold Sédar Senghor. Continue as a class to explore the importance of music in oral tradition and folklore.

### Teaching Tips

If students of African origin are in the French class, they may have access to more music and actual instruments. These students could make presentations on their favorite singers.

## LA LÉGENDE BAOULÉ
*Activity 6 (Days 9–10)*

### Preview

Have students locate Côte d'Ivoire on a map of Africa, and then show them an illustration of its major language groups (from the map used in Activity 2). Baoulé is in the Akan group of languages in the central part of the country. This activity introduces folktales, or contes. The folktale that is the focus of this activity is about *le peuple baoulé,* one of the ethnic groups in this area. The legend describes how this people got their name.

Have students read information about the author of the story, Bernard Dadié, on Handout 1, which also contains pictures of a famous Ivoirian stamp of Queen Pokou. You may want to supplement the handout with information students find on the web. Ask students to predict what Queen Pokou might have sacrificed as told in this legend.

### Focused Learning

Before reading the folktale *La Légende baoulé,* students need to review or learn African-specific vocabulary mentioned in the legend. Distribute Handout 2a, a list of vocabulary from the story, and Handout 2b, an exercise that asks students to classify this vocabulary into categories, such as animals, nature, insects, clothing, sounds, and actions. Have students work on this task in pairs. Review the answers in class (using the Teacher Key for Handout 2b, on the CD), and have students study these lexical items as homework to prepare for reading the folktale.

The class should read the entire legend aloud (taking turns) to simulate oral tradition. As an optional exercise, after the first reading, play an audio clip of Lamine Konté singing the story, while students listen and follow along, to simulate a more realistic rendering of traditional storytelling.

Discuss what students think is the message or moral contained in the story (e.g., *Il faut toujours sacrifier le bien individuel pour le bien de la société*). How does this reflect traditional African community values? As a formative assessment, have students complete the reading comprehension questions (Handout 3) for homework or as an in-class assignment.

### Expansion

Have students read other typical African folktales, or *contes*, and determine the cultural values or traditions that are presented. What role do animals or nature play? (See Supplementary Resources for additional folktales.)

### Teaching Tips

Make the reading of the legend as interactive as possible. The African audience often responds chorally, especially in refrains, so encourage students to join together orally in the refrain section. If a drum is available, they could lightly beat out a rhythm while the story is being read aloud.

## STRUCTURE PRACTICE IN FOLKTALES
*Activity 7 (Days 11–12)*

### Preview

Review the comprehension questions on *La Légende baoulé* completed for homework or as an in-class assignment (Handout 3 in Activity 6). Ask students what they think is the main message of the folktale.

### Focused Learning

Using the legend, review the use of the *imparfait* and the *passé simple*. Have students substitute the *passé composé* for verbs written in the *passé simple* in the story. Then have students complete an activity sheet on verb tenses (Handout 1). If students need more practice on verb tenses, assign activities from a grammar workbook. Additional verb drills are also available on numerous grammar practice websites, such as Quia (www.quia.com).

Using the legend as a basis, discuss how the author uses transition words and time words to enhance the story. In small groups, have students make a list of ones they find and then complete Handout 2. Remind students that they will need to use these words in a future writing assignment. Review the answers for Handouts 1 and 2 in class, using the teacher keys.

### Expansion

The class can read other folktales and look for the grammatical and structural features in these stories. The moral of each tale and the traditional cultural messages it portrays should also be discussed. In addition, francophone students from other countries can share folktales from their regions. Technology-enriched activities expand students' knowledge and understanding of the genre of folktales and how culture is integral to such tales. Numerous books and websites are available where students can find African folktales to read. See Supplementary Resources for some ideas.

### Teaching Tips

The verb tenses should be quite familiar by this level, but students always need practice with transition words and other discourse features found in folktales and other literature. They should apply these to their own creative writing. Students may keep a running list of such terms to help with writing activities.

## COMPARISON OF FOLKTALES: *LE PAGNE NOIR*
*Activity 8 (Day 13)*

### Preview

The main objective of Activities 8 and 9 is to have students compare a similar folktale in African and European contexts. Students will read another folktale by Bernard Dadié, *Le Pagne noir.* This African tale is very similar to the Grimm version of *Cinderella,* and students should begin to look for comparisons as they read. Explain to students that *Le Pagne noir* was written down in French by Dadié and published in 1955. However, the oral tradition of this story has existed for centuries in several African languages. Cinderella also has hundreds of versions in various languages.

If necessary, review the use of past tenses in narratives. Using the next two stories in this unit, *Le Pagne noir* and *Cendrillon*, students should continue to practice textual cohesive devices (transition words, adverbs of time, and story formulas—once upon a time, etc.) in preparation for their summative assessment or final project.

Have students engage in a pre-reading vocabulary task to make sure the African terms found in this story are understood (Handout 1a). Introduce the main characters and their traits, which students may recognize as those of Cinderella and the wicked stepmother.

### Focused Learning

Have students read *Le Pagne noir*, preferably aloud in class in the oral tradition. (The story is included on the CD.) Assign as homework the reading comprehension questions on Handout 1b. Handout 1c can be used as a springboard for discussion after the comprehension questions are corrected in class. As a formative assessment, have students select one of the topics suggested on Handout 1c for a short writing sample (at least one paragraph). They should include new African vocabulary learned, correct verb tenses, and transition words.

### Expansion

Show the film of the African folktale *Kirikou et la sorcière,* based on the children's book (which has beautiful illustrations and music by Youssou N'Dour). A study guide is available with numerous activities, such as comparing *Kirikou* to one of the Disney films (see Supplementary Resources).

### Teaching Tips

Focus on the unfamiliar African vocabulary as necessary. Have students develop a personalized vocabulary list that they can use throughout the unit. A wiki is a great repository for vocabulary lists.

## COMPARISON OF FOLKTALES: *CENDRILLON*
*Activity 9 (Day 14)*

### Preview

To start the activity, encourage students to predict the similarities to *Le Pagne noir* they will find in the Grimm brothers' version of *Cendrillon*. It is less familiar to students, but more similar to *Le Pagne noir* than the French Perrault version of *Cendrillon*, written around 1671. Explain to students that the Grimm version was written in German and published around 1812. The Grimm story *Cendrillon* is included on the CD (as Activity 9) and is also available online at www.chez.com/feeclochette/grimm.htm. The Perrault version is available at www.alalettre.com/perrault-cendrillon.htm.

You may want to prepare a pre-reading vocabulary review for antiquated or unusual words found in this version of the story.

### Focused Learning

Have students read the Grimm version of *Cendrillon*. You may wish to prepare reading comprehension questions to help guide students in this task. Then brainstorm with students the similarities (and differences) of the two tales, *Cendrillon* and *Le Pagne noir*. Distribute a comparison chart (Handout 2). Have students complete the chart, working in pairs or small groups, and then report back to the whole class for discussion and observations.

### Expansion

Discuss how these stories relate to folktales from other regions of the world studied in English literature classes. Ask students to reflect on why we find wicked stepmothers, wicked stepsisters, and "good girls" in so many stories from different cultures, times, and places. What elements (such as nature and animals) are similar in folktales and oral traditions from around the world? Why?

This is a good time to begin a class blog if you haven't started one yet.

### Teaching Tips

Before the summative assessment, it may be helpful for students to form study groups to review the essentials learned about folktales and oral tradition in this unit. Review of transition words and verb tenses is also important.

## OBJECTIVES FOR ACTIVITY 10
*(Days 15–18)*

### Content

Students will be able to:

- Write an original folktale based on the elements of this genre that have been studied.
- Explain the cultural message or moral used in the folktale.

### Language

Students will be able to:

- Use language appropriate to storytelling, including appropriate verb tenses, transition words, and adverbs of time.
- Describe cultural differences.

### Technology

Students will be able to:

- Use technology productivity tools—concept mapping software (e.g., Inspiration) to organize ideas and a word processor for writing.

- Use communication tools to share their product with others.

## CONTE ORIGINAL (ORIGINAL FOLKTALE)

*Activity 10 (Day 14)*

### Preview

As a summative assessment, students will write an original folktale that includes the cultural and structural features studied during this unit. The procedure for the entire summative assessment is provided for students in French on the CD (Handout 1).

To begin the activity, distribute Handout 1 and go over any questions. Have students read several African folktales, then meet in small groups to determine a list of traditional cultural values and/or moral messages that they believe are important to pass on to younger generations. These cultural values may be from students' own heritage groups (African, American, Chinese, Hispanic, Vietnamese, and so forth). Have student groups report to each other using a jigsaw or other grouping activity.

Students will determine which traditional value or moral message they wish to write about after listening to each other's ideas (and perhaps after checking with their families). Have each student write his or her proposed topic on an index card or e-mail and submit it to you for approval. After the topic has been approved, students can begin work on their plan, including setting, plot, and characters, using a program such as Inspiration.

Be sure to give students a writing rubric and remind them to check for the correct use of verb tenses and the inclusion of transition words and adverbs of time in their traditional story. Students must understand the story is to be original with specific cultural traits.

### Focused Learning

Instruct students to prewrite the original story in folktale format using a word processor. They can finish the first draft at home, submit it to you by e-mail, and prepare (or look for) at least one illustration using a graphics program. The following day students should participate in peer-editing and a discussion of the first draft in pairs. Have students edit the work accordingly and make final revisions at home, after they have seen the teacher's feedback.

The last day of the project, have students present their original folktales orally (preferably in small groups). Direct the members of the audience to write down what they believe is the message or moral of each student's folktale.

### Expansion

Numerous expansion activities are possible, depending on the time available and students' interests. A follow-up tech-based activity may include a joint online student publication that posts the folktales created by the class on a bulletin board or on student blogs. Students can videotape or make a sound recording of their original tale. If digital video cameras are available, students may incorporate original video clips into their presentations. They may also choose to publish a collection of the classes' tales using a word processor, presentation software, a multimedia authoring tool, or a blog.

To meet Foreign Language Standard 5.1, students should use the language both within and beyond the school setting. To accomplish this, groups of students could present their stories (or dialogues created from them) to other French classes, at a French club meeting, or, using videoconferencing, to an audience of students in a Francophone country. Another idea is to have students present at a cultural evening or heritage festival organized by the school or the community.

## UNIT EXTENSION AND TEACHING TIPS

### Unit Extension Activities

If time permits, students could explore more extended texts of African literature, such as *L'Enfant noir* (by Camara Laye) or *Une si longue lettre* (by Miriama Bâ). These works are included on the AP French literature list. Teachers will easily find these texts and study guides to accompany these works. Sources and additional authors are provided in Supplementary Resources. Technology-enriched activities could include online research about the authors and their works, followed by student oral or written presentations, using technology such as PowerPoint or Google Presentations, if desired.

African proverbs and sayings are a rich source of cultural knowledge. Using the Réseau Ivoire website (www.rezo-ivoire.net/littérature/citation.asp) and others found with online searches, students may select a few African proverbs and sayings for further investigation. Students will be able to expand their understanding and knowledge of African cultural values gained by studying African folktales through the exploration and interpretation of various proverbs. Comparisons can also be made with French, Canadian, Belgian, Haitian, or Swiss proverbs.

## Unit Teaching Tips

In our school, we have found a systematic way to address social, ethical, and human issues with an official International Baccalaureate course called Information Technology in a Global Society (ITGS). The ITGS course, taught in English, examines the social and ethical dimensions of technology use. Students work individually and in groups to find online articles about contemporary technology and social issues, such as legal and illegal music downloads; the paralanguage that has evolved for e-mail, chat, and instant messages; the censoring of web content by countries such as China; and the widening technology gap in developing countries (especially those in francophone Africa).

The latter topic—the widening technology gap in the developing world—is also addressed in a unit in a French textbook we use, *Collage: Varitiés Culturelles* (McGraw-Hill Higher Education, 2001). Based on an article reprinted from *L'Express,* "Tous égaux face au Web?" (Coste, 2000), this unit examines the social and human impact of the lack of technology access in poorer countries around the world. This unit engages French students in a healthy debate about the rich and the poor and how access to technology, and thus to information, leads to power. Many of our immigrant students from these regions of the world are concerned about this imbalance of power and are eager to explore ways they can help bridge the gap and be advocates for the *have nots.*

While it may be difficult for content area teachers to formally assess many of the NETS•S, foreign language teachers who regularly incorporate technology into their instruction and into student projects can evaluate their students' ability to use certain technologies to complete course content and language requirements by using a technology rubric (such as that provided for this unit) as part of their assessment.

ACTFL Standard 5.2, which requires students to demonstrate evidence of becoming lifelong learners by using the language for personal enjoyment, is also typically difficult for teachers to measure. One possible way to do this is to ask students to find a French speaker in their neighborhood or online and share a personal story with that person. If students post an original story on a blog or website, they may also attract some hits from francophone readers that they can document or present anecdotally to the rest of the classroom, providing teachers with some data on this standard.

# ASSESSING THE UNIT

## UNIT ASSESSMENTS

Formative and summative assessment measures are included throughout the unit. See the assessment materials provided on the CD.

## ASSESSMENT CRITERIA

Rubrics for most of the assessment tasks in this unit are provided on the CD as well as in Appendix A. Units 3 and 4 share the same assessment rubrics: Rubric for Oral Presentation, Rubric for Assessment of National Foreign Language Standards, and Rubric for Assessment of NETS•S. A rubric for assessing writing is not included with the Unit 4 rubrics. You might consider using or adapting the Rubric for Written Version of Presentation from Appendix A, Unit 1.

# APPENDIXES

# Assessment Rubrics for the Resource Units

The following rubrics may be used in conjunction with the assessment ideas outlined for each unit. **The accompanying CD has printable versions of these rubrics.**

## CoBaLTT Project
Content-Based Language Teaching with Technology

### Unit 1   Le Moyen Âge en France

- Rubric for Oral Presentation
- Rubric for Written Version of Presentation
- Rubric for Assessment of NETS·S—Technology Use for Final Project
- Rubric for Skit (from Activity 4)

### Unit 2   Les Stéréotypes des Français

- Rubric for NETS·S Assessment—Multimedia Presentation Project
- Rubric for Final Project

## Iowa State
The National K–12 Foreign Language Resource Center

### Unit 3   Carole Fredericks: Music Is Only the Beginning

### Unit 4   The Culture and Literature of Francophone West Africa

- Rubric for Oral Presentation
- Rubric for Assessment of NETS·S
- Rubric for Assessment of National Foreign Language Standards

## UNIT 1 ■ Le Moyen Âge en France

# RUBRIC FOR ORAL PRESENTATION

| CRITERIA | EXCEEDS EXPECTATIONS (9–10) | MEETS EXPECTATIONS (8–8.9) | NEEDS IMPROVEMENT (<8) POINTS | POINTS |
|---|---|---|---|---|
| Content | Presentation includes all required elements as well as additional information.<br><br>Examples demonstrate a depth of understanding that extends and challenges listeners' thinking.<br><br>Presentation is well organized and cohesive.<br><br>Presenter demonstrates in-depth knowledge of the topic. | Presentation includes all required elements.<br><br>Examples include sufficient detail for listeners to grasp the ideas presented.<br><br>Presentation is somewhat well organized and cohesive.<br><br>Presenter demonstrates accurate knowledge of the topic. | Presentation does not include all required elements.<br><br>Examples need additional detail for comprehension of the ideas presented.<br><br>Presentation needs additional organization and cohesiveness.<br><br>Presenter demonstrates limited knowledge of the topic. | ____ x 15 =<br><br>____ points |
| Language Control | Language (vocabulary and linguistic structures) is consistently accurate.<br><br>Vocabulary and linguistic structures are varied and sophisticated beyond the level of the class.<br><br>Use of *imparfait* and *passé composé* is always accurate. | Language (vocabulary and linguistic structures) is sufficiently accurate to ensure comprehension.<br><br>Vocabulary and linguistic structures are adequate for the level of the class.<br><br>Use of *imparfait* and *passé composé* is accurate most of the time. | Language (vocabulary and linguistic structures) is not sufficiently accurate to ensure comprehension.<br><br>Vocabulary and linguistic structures are not adequate for the level of the class.<br><br>Use of *imparfait* and *passé composé* is frequently inaccurate. | ____ x 10 =<br><br>____ points |
| Delivery | Presentation is well rehearsed and is presented confidently.<br><br>Student speaks consistently clearly with appropriate volume throughout the presentation.<br><br>Speaker makes eye contact consistently.<br><br>Visual enhances presentation.<br><br>Notes are used as an aid, but not read.<br><br>Speaker is able to elaborate examples clearly, with confidence and depth. | Presentation is rehearsed and is presented with some confidence.<br><br>Student speaks consistently clearly with appropriate volume most of the time.<br><br>Speaker makes eye contact some of the time.<br><br>Visual is adequate.<br><br>Notes are used as an aid and are occasionally read.<br><br>Speaker is able to explain examples adequately. | Presentation needs additional rehearsal to be presented confidently.<br><br>Student does not speak clearly with appropriate volume.<br><br>Speaker does not consistently make eye contact.<br><br>Visual is not adequate.<br><br>Speaker depends often on notes.<br><br>Speaker has difficulty explaining examples. | ____ x 5 =<br><br>____ points |
| GRADE: A = 94–100%; A- = 90–93%; B+ = 87–89%; B = 84–86%; B- = 80–83%; C+ = 77–79%; C = 74–76% | | | | Total:<br>____/300 |

UNIT 1 ▪ **Le Moyen Âge en France**

## RUBRIC FOR WRITTEN VERSION OF PRESENTATION

| CRITERIA | EXCEEDS EXPECTATIONS (9–10) | MEETS EXPECTATIONS (8–8.9) | NEEDS IMPROVEMENT (<8) POINTS | POINTS |
|---|---|---|---|---|
| Content | Speech includes all required elements as well as additional information.<br><br>Examples demonstrate a depth of understanding that extends and challenges listeners' thinking.<br><br>Speech is well organized and cohesive.<br><br>Writer demonstrates in-depth knowledge of the topic. | Speech includes all required elements.<br><br>Examples include sufficient detail for listeners to grasp the ideas presented.<br><br>Speech is somewhat well organized and cohesive.<br><br>Writer demonstrates accurate knowledge of the topic. | Speech does not include all required elements.<br><br>Examples need additional detail for listeners to grasp the ideas presented.<br><br>Speech needs additional organization and cohesiveness.<br><br>Writer demonstrates limited knowledge of the topic. | ___ x 15 = ___ points |
| Language Control | Language (vocabulary and linguistic structures) is consistently accurate.<br><br>Vocabulary and linguistic structures are varied and sophisticated beyond the level of the class.<br><br>Use of *imparfait* and *passé composé* is always accurate. | Language (vocabulary and linguistic structures) is sufficiently accurate to ensure comprehension.<br><br>Vocabulary and linguistic structures are adequate for the level of the class.<br><br>Use of *imparfait* and *passé composé* is accurate most of the time. | Language (vocabulary and linguistic structures) is not sufficiently accurate to ensure comprehension.<br><br>Vocabulary and linguistic structures are not adequate for the level of the class.<br><br>Use of *imparfait* and *passé composé* is frequently inaccurate. | ___ x 15 = ___ points |

| GRADE: A = 94–100%; A- = 90–93%; B+ = 87–89%; B = 84–86%; B- = 80–83%; C+ = 77–79%; C = 74–76% | Total: ___/300 |
|---|---|

## UNIT 1 ▪ Le Moyen Âge en France

# RUBRIC FOR ASSESSMENT OF NETS·S—TECHNOLOGY USE FOR FINAL PROJECT

| CRITERIA | EXCEEDS EXPECTATIONS (9–10) | MEETS EXPECTATIONS (8–8.9) | NEEDS IMPROVEMENT (<8) POINTS | POINTS |
|---|---|---|---|---|
| **1. Creativity and Innovation** Students demonstrate creative thinking, construct knowledge, and develop innovative products and processes using technology. Students: **a.** apply existing knowledge to generate new ideas, products, or processes. **b.** create original works as a means of personal or group expression. | Multimedia authoring tools were used beyond expectations. The applications of their use go beyond the requirements of the project and greatly enhanced the effectiveness of the oral presentation. Many illustrations were provided and the slides were organized in a clear and logical manner. | Multimedia authoring tools were used with the minimum proficiency required to produce an acceptable oral presentation. Some illustrations were provided and the overall presentation was easy to follow. | Multimedia authoring tools were used with an obvious lack of the proficiency required to support the oral presentation. The overall presentation suffered from the use of the tools rather than being supported by them. No illustrations were provided and the slides did not have a logical flow. | ____ x 15 = ____ points |
| **2. Communication and Collaboration (for those attempting to score extra points)** Students use digital media and environments to communicate and work collaboratively, including at a distance, to support individual learning and contribute to the learning of others. Students: **a.** interact, collaborate, and publish with peers, experts, or others employing a variety of digital environments and media. **b.** communicate information and ideas effectively to multiple audiences using a variety of media and formats. **c.** develop cultural understanding and global awareness by engaging with learners of other cultures. **d.** contribute to project teams to produce original works or solve problems. | Communication tools were used beyond expectations. Students not only showed a very good control over the use of these tools but also applied their use in ways that exceed the requirements of this project. Students were successful in establishing communication with others. | Communication tools were used with the proficiency necessary to communicate with others. The use of the tools is acceptable and remains in the realm of "expected" usage. Students were not successful in establishing communication with others even though they repeatedly attempted to. | Communication tools were used unsuccessfully and their use shows a lack of the proficiency necessary to communicate with others. Students failed in their attempt to establish communication with others and abandoned their quest without further effort. | ____ x 5 = ____ points |

| CRITERIA | EXCEEDS EXPECTATIONS (9–10) | MEETS EXPECTATIONS (8–8.9) | NEEDS IMPROVEMENT (<8) POINTS | POINTS |
|---|---|---|---|---|
| **3. Research and Information Fluency**<br><br>Students apply digital tools to gather, evaluate, and use information. Students:<br><br>**b.** locate, organize, analyze, evaluate, synthesize, and ethically use information from a variety of sources and media.<br><br>**c.** evaluate and select information sources and digital tools based on the appropriateness to specific tasks. | Students went beyond the minimum proficiency for using research tools and applied their use beyond the requirements of this project. | Students met the minimum proficiency for using research tools. Students identified useful websites and gathered interesting material that helped them complete their project. | Students did not meet the minimum proficiency for using research tools. Students failed to identify useful websites or gather interesting material that could help them complete their project. | ____ x 10 =<br><br>____ points |
| **GRADE:** A = 94–100%; A- = 90–93%; B+ = 87–89%; B = 84–86%; B- = 80–83%; C+ = 77–79%; C = 74–76% | | | | Total:<br>____ /300<br>Bonus: ____ |

## UNIT 1 ▪ Le Moyen Âge en France

## RUBRIC FOR SKIT (from Activity 4)

| CRITERIA | EXCEEDS EXPECTATIONS (9–10) | MEETS EXPECTATIONS (8–8.9) | NEEDS IMPROVEMENT (<8) POINTS | POINTS |
|---|---|---|---|---|
| Content | Introduction includes all required elements as well as additional information.<br><br>Presenters demonstrate in-depth knowledge of the topic.<br><br>Excerpt chosen allows class to easily understand the story.<br><br>Presentation is well organized and cohesive.<br><br>Skit shows excellent creativity. | Introduction includes all required elements.<br><br>Presenters demonstrate accurate knowledge of the topic.<br><br>Excerpt chosen allows class to understand the story.<br><br>Presentation is somewhat well organized and cohesive.<br><br>Skit shows creativity. | Introduction does not include all required elements.<br><br>Presenters demonstrate limited knowledge of the topic.<br><br>Excerpt chosen does not allow class to understand the story adequately.<br><br>Presentation needs additional organization and cohesiveness.<br><br>Skit shows limited creativity. | ____ x 15 =<br><br>____ points |
| Language Control | Language (vocabulary and linguistic structures) is consistently accurate.<br><br>Vocabulary and linguistic structures are varied and sophisticated beyond the level of the class.<br><br>Use of *imparfait* and *passé composé* is always accurate. | Language (vocabulary and linguistic structures) is sufficiently accurate to ensure comprehension.<br><br>Vocabulary and linguistic structures are adequate for the level of the class.<br><br>Use of *imparfait* and *passé composé* is accurate most of the time. | Language (vocabulary and linguistic structures) is not sufficiently accurate to ensure comprehension.<br><br>Vocabulary and linguistic structures are not adequate for the level of the class.<br><br>Use of *imparfait* and *passé composé* is frequently inaccurate. | ____ x 5 =<br><br>____ points |
| Delivery | Presentation is very well rehearsed and is delivered very confidently and expressively.<br><br>Students speak consistently clearly with appropriate volume throughout the presentation.<br><br>Notes are used as an aid, but not read.<br><br>Presenters are very animated and use excellent gestures and movement. | Presentation is rehearsed and is delivered with some confidence and expression.<br><br>Students speak consistently clearly with appropriate volume most of the time.<br><br>Notes are used as an aid and are occasionally read.<br><br>Presenters are somewhat animated and use some gestures and movement. | Presentation needs additional rehearsal to be delivered confidently and expressively.<br><br>Students do not speak clearly with appropriate volume.<br><br>Speakers depend often on notes.<br><br>Presenters lack animation, gestures, and movement. | ____ x 10 =<br><br>____ points |
| **GRADE:** A = 94–100%; A- = 90–93%; B+ = 87–89%; B = 84–86%; B- = 80–83%; C+ = 77–79%; C = 74–76% | | | | Total:<br>____/300 |

UNIT 2 ▪ Les Stéréotypes des Français

# RUBRIC FOR NETS·S ASSESSMENT—MULTIMEDIA PRESENTATION PROJECT

| CRITERIA | EXCEEDS EXPECTATIONS 3 | MEETS EXPECTATIONS 2 | NEEDS IMPROVEMENT 1 | SCORE |
|---|---|---|---|---|
| **1. Creativity and Innovation**<br><br>Students demonstrate creative thinking, construct knowledge, and develop innovative products and processes using technology. Students:<br><br>**a.** apply existing knowledge to generate new ideas, products, or processes.<br><br>**b.** create original works as a means of personal or group expression. | Presentation shows considerable originality and inventiveness. The content and ideas were presented in a unique and interesting way.<br><br>Students make excellent use of font, color, graphics, effects, and other elements to enhance the presentation. | Presentation shows some originality and inventiveness. The content and ideas were presented in an interesting way.<br><br>Students make use of font, color, graphics, effects, and other elements to enhance the presentation but at times they fail to enhance it and seem unnecessary. | Presentation shows little or no originality and very little attempt at inventiveness. The content and ideas were not presented in an interesting way.<br><br>Students make some use of font, color, graphics, effects, and other elements, but these often distract from the presentation content. | |
| **3. Research and Information Fluency**<br><br>Students apply digital tools to gather, evaluate, and use information. Students:<br><br>**b.** locate, organize, analyze, evaluate, synthesize, and ethically use information from a variety of sources and media.<br><br>**c.** evaluate and select information sources and digital tools based on the appropriateness to specific tasks. | Students went beyond the minimum proficiency for using research tools and applied their use beyond the requirements for this project. | Students met the minimum proficiency for using research tools. Students identified useful websites and gathered interesting material that helped them complete their project. | Students did not meet the minimum proficiency for using research tools. Students failed to identify useful websites or gather material that could help them complete their project. | |
| **6. Technology Operations and Concepts**<br><br>Students demonstrate a sound understanding of technology concepts, systems, and operations. Students:<br><br>**a.** understand and use technology systems.<br><br>**b.** select and use applications effectively and productively. | Students have an exceptional understanding of the technological tools, allowing them to go beyond expectations.<br><br>All the required outputs were produced in the precise format requested.<br><br>Students can easily answer questions about the content and procedures used to make the multimedia presentation. | Students have a fair understanding of the technological tools, allowing them to meet expectations.<br><br>Most of the required outputs were produced although some may not have been exactly in the expected format.<br><br>Students can answer most questions about the content and procedures used to make the multimedia presentation but may falter with some. | Students have a limited understanding of the technological tools.<br><br>Few if any of the required outputs were produced and/or they were not in the expected format.<br><br>Students can answer very few questions about the content and procedures used to make the multimedia presentation. | |

## UNIT 2 ▪ Les Stéréotypes des Français

# RUBRIC FOR FINAL PROJECT

| CRITERIA | EXCELLENT 4 | GOOD 3 | ACCEPTABLE 2 | NEEDS IMPROVEMENT 1 |
|---|---|---|---|---|
| Development, Organization, and Visuals | Presentation is well developed and well organized; listeners are able to follow along easily. Visuals are excellent and enhance the content of the presentation. | Presentation is somewhat developed and organized; listeners can follow most of it without difficulty. Visuals enhance the content of the presentation to some extent. | Presentation development and organization are uneven; important links may be missing and it is difficult for listeners to follow. Visuals seem peripheral and are not well integrated. | Presentation is undeveloped, unorganized, and disconnected, making it very difficult for listeners to follow. Visuals are lacking, are not integrated, or do not support the presentation. |
| Communication of Key Concepts | Presentation reflects strong understanding of the key concepts related to stereotypes. Examples clearly illustrate the concepts. | Presentation reflects good understanding of the key concepts related to stereotypes. Examples generally illustrate the concepts. | Presentation reflects some understanding of the key concepts related to stereotypes. Examples do not always clearly illustrate the concepts. | Presentation does not reflect understanding of the key concepts related to stereotypes. Examples are lacking. |
| Vocabulary and Language Use | Use of a wide range of topic-specific vocabulary; clear communication of ideas; mostly accurate use of tenses, word order. Some compound sentences included. | Use of a good range of topic-specific vocabulary; good communication of ideas; good control of tenses, word order. Some compound sentences attempted. | Lacking some critical topic-specific vocabulary; limited range of words; errors in tenses and word order at times impede understanding. Only simple sentences are included. | Vocabulary is limited and at times inappropriate, which occasionally impedes comprehension. Consistently inaccurate use of tenses and word order. Sentences are incomplete. |
| Pronunciation, Fluency, and Eye Contact | Pronunciation and intonation are level-appropriate. Smooth and fluent speech indicates evidence of rehearsal. Excellent eye contact with the audience. | Always intelligible, though there may be a noticeable accent and lapses in intonation. Speech mostly smooth, reflecting some rehearsal. Eyes mostly focused on audience. | Pronunciation problems partially impede comprehensibility. Speech is hesitant, showing little evidence of rehearsal (some reading of slides). Eyes focus more on notes rather than on audience. | Very difficult to follow due to pronunciation problems. Speech is slow with many pauses, showing no evidence of rehearsal (slides mostly read). Eyes focus on slides and notes. |
| Participation and Group Work | Each group member assumes an equal and active role in the preparation and presentation. | Each group member assumes a role, although some members appear more active or responsible for a majority of the work. | Participation among group members is uneven; some students are passive and contribute little to the presentation. | Some students hardly participate; no effort is made to distribute work among all group members. |

**Non-negotiable items for Unit 2 final project:**

- All group members must participate in the slideshow preparation and oral presentation.

- All required components of the presentation must be included.

- A minimum of nine slides must be used.

- The written commentary that accompanies each slide must be turned in.

- A description of each individual's contribution to the group effort must be submitted (in English).

UNIT 3 ▪ **Carole Fredericks: Music Is Only the Beginning**
UNIT 4 ▪ **The Culture and Literature of Francophone West Africa**

# RUBRIC FOR ORAL PRESENTATION

| CRITERIA | EXCELLENT 4 | GOOD 3 | ACCEPTABLE 2 | NEEDS IMPROVEMENT 1 |
|---|---|---|---|---|
| Comprehension | Student is able to accurately answer almost all questions posed by classmates about the topic. | Student is able to accurately answer most questions posed by classmates about the topic. | Student is able to accurately answer a few questions posed by classmates about the topic. | Student is unable to accurately answer questions posed by classmates about the topic. |
| Preparedness | Student is completely prepared and has obviously rehearsed. | Student seems pretty prepared but might have needed a couple more rehearsals. | Student is somewhat prepared, but it is clear that rehearsal was lacking. | Student does not seem at all prepared to present. |
| Content | Student shows a full understanding of the topic. | Student shows a good understanding of the topic. | Student shows a good understanding of parts of the topic. | Student does not seem to understand the topic very well. |
| Attention to Other Presentations | Student listens intently and does not make distracting noises or movements. | Student listens intently but has one distracting noise or movement. | Student sometimes does not appear to be listening but is not distracting. | Student sometimes does not appear to be listening and has distracting noises or movements. |
| Enunciation | Student speaks clearly and distinctly all (95–100%) the time, and mispronounces no words. | Student speaks clearly and distinctly all (95–100%) the time, but mispronounces one word. | Student speaks clearly and distinctly most (85–94%) of the time and mispronounces no more than one word. | Student often mumbles or cannot be understood or mispronounces more than one word. |
| Vocabulary | Student uses vocabulary appropriate for the audience. Student extends the audience vocabulary by defining words that might be new to most of the audience. | Student uses vocabulary appropriate for the audience. Student includes 1–2 words that might be new to most of the audience, but does not define them. | Student uses vocabulary appropriate for the audience. Student does not include any vocabulary that might be new to the audience. | Student uses several (5 or more) words or phrases that are not understood by the audience. |
| Complete Sentences | Student always (99–100% of the time) speaks in complete sentences. | Student mostly (80–98% of the time) speaks in complete sentences. | Student sometimes (70–79% of the time) speaks in complete sentences. | Student rarely speaks in complete sentences. |

UNIT 3 ▪ Carole Fredericks: Music Is Only the Beginning
UNIT 4 ▪ The Culture and Literature of Francophone West Africa

## RUBRIC FOR ASSESSMENT OF NETS•S

| CRITERIA | EXCEEDS EXPECTATIONS 3 | MEETS EXPECTATIONS 2 | NEEDS IMPROVEMENT 1 |
|---|---|---|---|
| **1. Creativity and Innovation** Students demonstrate creative thinking, construct knowledge, and develop innovative products and processes using technology. Students: **a.** apply existing knowledge to generate new ideas, products, or processes. **b.** create original works as a means of personal or group expression. | Presentation shows considerable originality and inventiveness. The content and ideas were presented in a unique and interesting way. Students make excellent use of font, color, graphics, effects, and other elements to enhance the presentation. | Presentation shows some originality and inventiveness. The content and ideas were presented in an interesting way. Students make use of font, color, graphics, effects, and other elements to enhance the presentation but at times they fail to enhance it and seem unnecessary. | Presentation shows little or no originality and very little attempt at inventiveness. The content and ideas were not presented in an interesting way. Students make some use of font, color, graphics, effects, and other elements, but these often distract from the presentation content. |
| **3. Research and Information Fluency** Students apply digital tools to gather, evaluate, and use information. Students: **b.** locate, organize, analyze, evaluate, synthesize, and ethically use information from a variety of sources and media. **c.** evaluate and select information sources and digital tools based on the appropriateness to specific tasks. | Students went beyond the minimum proficiency for using research tools and applied their use beyond the requirements for this project. | Students met the minimum proficiency for using research tools. Students identified useful websites and gathered interesting material that helped them complete their project. | Students did not meet the minimum proficiency for using research tools. Students failed to identify useful websites or gather material that could help them complete their project. |
| **6. Technology Operations and Concepts** Students demonstrate a sound understanding of technology concepts, systems, and operations. Students: **b.** select and use applications effectively and productively. | Students have an exceptional understanding of the technological tools, allowing them to go beyond expectations. All the required outputs were produced in the precise format requested. Students can easily answer questions about the content and procedures used to make the multimedia presentation. | Students have a fair understanding of the technological tools, allowing them to meet expectations. Most of the required outputs were produced although some may not have been exactly in the expected format. Students can answer most questions about the content and procedures used to make the multimedia presentation but may falter with some. | Students have a limited understanding of the technological tools. Few if any of the required outputs were produced and/or they were not in the expected format. Students can answer very few questions about the content and procedures used to make the multimedia presentation. |

UNIT 3 ▪ **Carole Fredericks: Music Is Only the Beginning**
UNIT 4 ▪ **The Culture and Literature of Francophone West Africa**

# RUBRIC FOR ASSESSMENT OF NATIONAL FOREIGN LANGUAGE STANDARDS

| CRITERIA | EXEMPLARY 3 | SATISFACTORY 2 | UNSATISFACTORY 1 | SCORE |
|---|---|---|---|---|
| 1.1. Students engage in conversations, provide and obtain information, express feelings and emotions, and exchange opinions. | Student demonstrates exemplary understanding, making connections to personal experience through higher-level applications of thinking. | Student demonstrates acceptable understanding within the context of the unit. | Understanding is not in evidence. | |
| 1.2. Students understand and interpret written and spoken language on a variety of topics. | Student demonstrates exemplary understanding, making connections to personal experience through higher-level applications of thinking. | Student demonstrates acceptable understanding within the context of the unit. | Understanding is not in evidence. | |
| 1.3. Students present information, concepts, and ideas to an audience of listeners or readers on a variety of topics. | Student demonstrates exemplary understanding, making connections to personal experience through higher-level applications of thinking. | Student demonstrates acceptable understanding within the context of the unit. | Understanding is not in evidence. | |
| 2.1. Students demonstrate an understanding of the relationship between the practices and perspective of the culture studied. | Student demonstrates exemplary understanding, making connections to personal experience through higher-level applications of thinking. | Student demonstrates acceptable understanding within the context of the unit. | Understanding is not in evidence. | |
| 2.2. Students demonstrate an understanding of the relationship between the products and perspectives of the culture studied. | Student demonstrates exemplary understanding, making connections to personal experience through higher-level applications of thinking. | Student demonstrates acceptable understanding within the context of the unit. | Understanding is not in evidence. | |

| CRITERIA | EXEMPLARY 3 | SATISFACTORY 2 | UNSATISFACTORY 1 | SCORE |
|---|---|---|---|---|
| **3.1.** Students reinforce and further their knowledge of other disciplines through the foreign language. | Student demonstrates exemplary understanding, making connections to personal experience through higher-level applications of thinking. | Student demonstrates acceptable understanding within the context of the unit. | Understanding is not in evidence. | |
| **3.2.** Students acquire information and recognize the distinctive viewpoints that are only available through the foreign language and its cultures. | Student demonstrates exemplary understanding, making connections to personal experience through higher-level applications of thinking. | Student demonstrates acceptable understanding within the context of the unit. | Understanding is not in evidence. | |
| **4.1.** Students demonstrate understanding of the nature of language through comparisons of the language studied and their own. | Student demonstrates exemplary understanding, making connections to personal experience through higher-level applications of thinking. | Student demonstrates acceptable understanding within the context of the unit. | Understanding is not in evidence. | |
| **4.2.** Students demonstrate understanding of the concept of culture through comparisons of the cultures studied and their own. | Student demonstrates exemplary understanding, making connections to personal experience through higher-level applications of thinking. | Student demonstrates acceptable understanding within the context of the unit. | Understanding is not in evidence. | |
| **5.1.** Students use the language both within and beyond the school setting. | Student demonstrates exemplary understanding, making connections to personal experience through higher-level applications of thinking. | Student demonstrates acceptable understanding within the context of the unit. | Understanding is not in evidence. | |
| **5.2.** Students show evidence of becoming life-long learners by using the language for personal enjoyment and enrichment. | Student demonstrates exemplary understanding, making connections to personal experience through higher-level applications of thinking. | Student demonstrates acceptable understanding within the context of the unit. | Understanding is not in evidence. | |

# Learn More
# with Additional Resources

## Take Your Foreign Language Classroom to the Next Level

ISTE advances excellence in learning and teaching through innovative and effective uses of technology. It is our belief that any educator can make a tremendous impact in student learning through the effective use of technology in the classroom. As part of our mission, we publish a plethora of books to help make it easy for you to adopt those technologies you feel will work for you and your students.

## Further Reading

As you read through the units and lesson plans included in this book, you will notice suggestions for incorporating technology. It is outside the scope of this book to teach you how to use each and every technology that is suggested. In this appendix, we discuss relevant resources that will introduce and teach you how to use the latest educational technologies.

*Digital Storytelling Guide for Educators* by Midge Frazel shows you how to teach your students to use text, music, sound effects, video, and more to create effective multimedia presentations. This book will show you how to teach your students to create meaningful presentations for authentic audiences—an especially effective strategy in the foreign language classroom. The author also discusses variations on digital storytelling, including e-portfolios, digital photo essays, and scrapblogs (www.iste.org/digsto).

*Global Education: Using Technology to Bring the World to Your Students* by Laurence Peters breaks down the walls of your classroom, connecting your students to communities of learners around the world, expanding their knowledge and awareness of other cultures, and increasing their interest and curiosity in what they are learning.

Foreign language students learn best when given ample opportunities to communicate meaningful content for real-world purposes and in real-world settings. Imagine partnering with a classroom in France, Sénégal, or Québec—this book will show you how to use existing, free global networks such as iEarn, Global Schoolhouse, and ePals to team up with other classrooms around the world for authentic interaction in the target language. Also discussed are Web 2.0 tools that support global learning (www.iste.org/global).

*Retool Your School: The Educator's Essential Guide to Google's Free Power Apps* by James Lerman and Ronique Hicks explores Google Apps, some of the best free online learning tools available today. Use Google Docs for collaborative writing, Google Sites to create class wikis, Google Presesentations for slide shows, Google Earth and Maps to explore the terrain of other countries, Google Forms and Spreadsheets to conduct surveys and analyze data, Picasa to store and share images, and Blogger to share writing and receive immediate feedback (www.iste.org/google).

*Student-Powered Podcasting: Teaching for 21st-Century Literacy* by Christopher Shamburg brings podcasting into the classroom, with students doing the creating. The author explains what podcasting is and why you should consider teaching it to your students. He leads you through two tutorials, one for PC and one for Macintosh, so you can jump in and start podcasting right away. Also included are 17 units that can be adapted for the foreign language classroom, including one specifically written for foreign language instruction. Podcasting is an ideal way to develop and practice speaking skills and reduce phobias associated with speaking in a foreign language (www.iste.org/podhum).

*Teaching with Digital Video,* edited by Glen L. Bull and Lynn Bell, covers all aspects of digital video use in the classroom. The editors describe the most effective ways to introduce video in the classroom to create engaged learners. They walk you through various means of acquiring appropriate video for instruction and provide advice on creating effective videos. Most importantly, the book emphasizes the importance of teaching your students how to be active, critical consumers of video (www.iste.org/digvid).

*Toys to Tools: Connecting Student Cell Phones to Education* by Liz Kolb recasts the humble cell phone as an effective tool for learning. In the foreign language classroom, student cell phones can be used to record and upload your students reading, reciting, conducting interviews, podcasting, and more (www.iste.org/toytul).

*Videoconferencing for K–12 Classrooms: A Program Development Guide* (2nd Edition) by Camille Cole, Kecia Ray, and Jan Zanetis explores the potential of interactive videoconferencing to link classrooms worldwide, connect far-flung learners to subject area experts, expose students to places and people that simply cannot be reached through traditional field trips, and bring in much-needed supplemental content. With videoconferencing, your students can engage directly with native speakers of the target language on a regular basis (www.iste.org/vidco2).

*Web 2.0: New Tools, New Schools* and *Web 2.0 How-To for Educators* by Gwen Solomon and Lynne Schrum introduce the world of Web 2.0 tools and how educators can best make use of them. Through blogging, students can write posts in the target language and receive immediate feedback from their classmates as well as others from around the world. Wikis are great repositories for vocabulary words, timelines, geographical information, and more. Foreign-language podcasts provide interesting content in the target language on a regular basis. These Web 2.0 tools, *Web 2.0: New Tools, New Schools* (www.iste.org/newtoo) and *Web 2.0 How-To for Educators (*www.iste.org/how2ns), and many more are easy to adopt in the foreign language classroom.

In addition to introducing you to a variety of educational technologies, many of these resources explore issues of student privacy, etiquette, and safety when using these tools. They provide you with strategies to keep your students safe, on task, and acting in an appropriate manner as they take advantage of all that educational technologies have to offer.

## Online Resources Suggested by ACTFL

CARLA Virtual Assessment Center
www.carla.umn.edu/assessment/vac/

Center for Applied Linguistics
www.cal.org

Companion site to *Teacher's Handbook: Contextualized Language Instruction*
http://thandbook.heinle.com

edweek.org—Current issues in education
www.edweek.org/ew/

FLTEACH: Foreign Language Methods Syllabi Archive
www.cortland.edu/flteach/syllabi/

Integrating New Technology into the Methods of Education
www.intime.uni.edu

Teaching Foreign Languages K–12: A Library of Classroom Practices
www.learner.org/channel/libraries/tfl/

Teaching Foreign Language K–12 Workshop
www.learner.org/resources/series201.html

Wikipedia: Second Language Acquisition Information
http://en.wikipedia.org/wiki/Second_language_acquisition

# Standards for Foreign Language Learning

T he national standards for foreign language education center around five goals: Communication, Cultures, Connections, Comparisons, and Communities— the five Cs of foreign language education.

## Communication
*Communicate in Languages Other Than English*

**Standard 1.1.** Students engage in conversations, provide and obtain information, express feelings and emotions, and exchange opinions.

**Standard 1.2.** Students understand and interpret written and spoken language on a variety of topics.

**Standard 1.3.** Students present information, concepts, and ideas to an audience of listeners or readers on a variety of topics.

## Cultures
*Gain Knowledge and Understanding of Other Cultures*

**Standard 2.1.** Students demonstrate an understanding of the relationship between the practices and perspectives of the culture studied.

**Standard 2.2.** Students demonstrate an understanding of the relationship between the products and perspectives of the culture studied.

## Connections

*Connect with Other Disciplines and Acquire Information*

**Standard 3.1.** Students reinforce and further their knowledge of other disciplines through the foreign language.

**Standard 3.2.** Students acquire information and recognize the distinctive viewpoints that are only available through the foreign language and its cultures.

## Comparisons

*Develop Insight into the Nature of Language and Culture*

**Standard 4.1.** Students demonstrate understanding of the nature of language through comparisons of the language studied and their own.

**Standard 4.2.** Students demonstrate understanding of the concept of culture through comparisons of the cultures studied and their own.

## Communities

*Participate in Multilingual Communities at Home and Around the World*

**Standard 5.1.** Students use the language both within and beyond the school setting.

**Standard 5.2.** Students show evidence of becoming life-long learners by using the language for personal enjoyment and enrichment.

*Reprinted with permission from the National Standards in Foreign Language Education Project.*

# APPENDIX D

# National Educational Technology Standards

Teachers know that the wise use of technology can enrich learning environments for students, and this is especially true in the foreign language classroom. However, successful learning activities, such as the ones provided in this book, depend on more than just technology for success. Certain conditions are necessary for schools to effectively use technology for learning, teaching, and educational management.

## The NETS Project

The National Educational Technology Standards (NETS) Project was initiated by the Accreditation and Professional Standards Committee of the International Society for Technology in Education (ISTE). ISTE has emerged as a recognized leader among professional organizations for educators involved with technology. ISTE's mission is to promote appropriate uses of technology to support and improve learning, teaching, and administration. Its members are leaders in educational technology, including teachers, technology coordinators, education administrators, and teacher educators. ISTE supports all subject area disciplines by providing publications, conferences, online resources, and services that help educators combine the knowledge and skills of their teaching fields with the application of technologies to improve learning and teaching.

The primary goal of the NETS Project is to enable stakeholders in PK–12 education to develop national standards for the educational uses of technology that facilitate school improvement in the United States. The NETS Project is developing standards to guide educational leaders in recognizing and addressing the essential conditions for the effective use of technology to support PK–12 education.

# Essential Conditions for Technology Integration

Physical, pedagogical, financial, and policy dimensions greatly affect the success of technology use in schools. The lessons provided in this book will be more effective if a combination of essential conditions for creating learning environments conducive to powerful uses of technology is achieved, including:

### Shared Vision

Proactive leadership in developing a shared vision for educational technology among all education stakeholders including teachers and support staff, school and district administrators, teacher educators, students, parents, and the community

### Empowered Leaders

Stakeholders at every level empowered to be leaders in effecting change

### Implementation Planning

A systematic plan aligned with a shared vision for school effectiveness and student learning through the infusion of information and communication technologies (ICT) and digital learning resources

### Consistent and Adequate Funding

Ongoing funding to support technology infrastructure, personnel, digital resources, and staff development

### Equitable Access

Robust and reliable access to current and emerging technologies and digital resources, with connectivity for all students, teachers, staff, and school leaders

### Skilled Personnel

Educators, support staff, and other leaders skilled in the selection and effective use of appropriate ICT resources

### Ongoing Professional Learning

Technology-related professional learning plans and opportunities with dedicated time to practice and share ideas

## Technical Support

Consistent and reliable assistance for maintaining, renewing, and using ICT and digital learning resources

## Curriculum Framework

Content standards and related digital curriculum resources that are aligned with and support digital-age learning and work

## Student-Centered Learning

Planning, teaching, and assessment centered around the needs and abilities of students

## Assessment and Evaluation

Continuous assessment of teaching, learning, and leadership, and evaluation of the use of ICT and digital resources

## Engaged Communities

Partnerships and collaboration within communities to support and fund the use of ICT and digital resources

## Support Policies

Policies, financial plans, accountability measures, and incentive structures to support the use of ICT and digital learning resources for learning and in district school operations

## Supportive External Context

Policies and initiatives at the national, regional, and local levels to support schools and teacher preparation programs in effective implementation of technology for achieving curriculum and learning technology (ICT) standards

*© 2008 International Society for Technology in Education (ISTE), www.iste.org. All rights reserved.*

# NETS for Students

All K–12 students should be prepared to meet the following standards and performance indicators:

### 1. Creativity and Innovation

Students demonstrate creative thinking, construct knowledge, and develop innovative products and processes using technology. Students:

  a.  apply existing knowledge to generate new ideas, products, or processes

  b.  create original works as a means of personal or group expression

  c.  use models and simulations to explore complex systems and issues

  d.  identify trends and forecast possibilities

### 2. Communication and Collaboration

Students use digital media and environments to communicate and work collaboratively, including at a distance, to support individual learning and contribute to the learning of others. Students:

  a.  interact, collaborate, and publish with peers, experts, or others employing a variety of digital environments and media

  b.  communicate information and ideas effectively to multiple audiences using a variety of media and formats

  c.  develop cultural understanding and global awareness by engaging with learners of other cultures

  d.  contribute to project teams to produce original works or solve problems

### 3. Research and Information Fluency

Students apply digital tools to gather, evaluate, and use information. Students:

  a.  plan strategies to guide inquiry

  b.  locate, organize, analyze, evaluate, synthesize, and ethically use information from a variety of sources and media

  c.  evaluate and select information sources and digital tools based on the appropriateness to specific tasks

  d.  process data and report results

## 4. Critical Thinking, Problem Solving, and Decision Making

Students use critical thinking skills to plan and conduct research, manage projects, solve problems, and make informed decisions using appropriate digital tools and resources. Students:

**a.** identify and define authentic problems and significant questions for investigation

**b.** plan and manage activities to develop a solution or complete a project

**c.** collect and analyze data to identify solutions and/or make informed decisions

**d.** use multiple processes and diverse perspectives to explore alternative solutions

## 5. Digital Citizenship

Students understand human, cultural, and societal issues related to technology and practice legal and ethical behavior. Students:

**a.** advocate and practice safe, legal, and responsible use of information and technology

**b.** exhibit a positive attitude toward using technology that supports collaboration, learning, and productivity

**c.** demonstrate personal responsibility for lifelong learning

**d.** exhibit leadership for digital citizenship

## 6. Technology Operations and Concepts

Students demonstrate a sound understanding of technology concepts, systems, and operations. Students:

**a.** understand and use technology systems

**b.** select and use applications effectively and productively

**c.** troubleshoot systems and applications

**d.** transfer current knowledge to learning of new technologies

© *2007 International Society for Technology in Education (ISTE), www.iste.org. All rights reserved.*

# NETS for Teachers

Effective teachers model and apply the National Educational Technology Standards for Students (NETS•S) as they design, implement, and assess learning experiences to engage students and improve learning; enrich professional practice; and provide positive models for students, colleagues, and the community. All teachers should meet the following standards and performance indicators. Teachers:

1. **Facilitate and Inspire Student Learning and Creativity**

   Teachers use their knowledge of subject matter, teaching and learning, and technology to facilitate experiences that advance student learning, creativity, and innovation in both face-to-face and virtual environments. Teachers:

   a. promote, support, and model creative and innovative thinking and inventiveness

   b. engage students in exploring real-world issues and solving authentic problems using digital tools and resources

   c. promote student reflection using collaborative tools to reveal and clarify students' conceptual understanding and thinking, planning, and creative processes

   d. model collaborative knowledge construction by engaging in learning with students, colleagues, and others in face-to-face and virtual environments

2. **Design and Develop Digital-Age Learning Experiences and Assessments**

   Teachers design, develop, and evaluate authentic learning experiences and assessments incorporating contemporary tools and resources to maximize content learning in context and to develop the knowledge, skills, and attitudes identified in the NETS•S. Teachers:

   a. design or adapt relevant learning experiences that incorporate digital tools and resources to promote student learning and creativity

   b. develop technology-enriched learning environments that enable all students to pursue their individual curiosities and become active participants in setting their own educational goals, managing their own learning, and assessing their own progress

   c. customize and personalize learning activities to address students' diverse learning styles, working strategies, and abilities using digital tools and resources

**d.** provide students with multiple and varied formative and summative assessments aligned with content and technology standards and use resulting data to inform learning and teaching

## 3. Model Digital-Age Work and Learning

Teachers exhibit knowledge, skills, and work processes representative of an innovative professional in a global and digital society. Teachers:

**a.** demonstrate fluency in technology systems and the transfer of current knowledge to new technologies and situations

**b.** collaborate with students, peers, parents, and community members using digital tools and resources to support student success and innovation

**c.** communicate relevant information and ideas effectively to students, parents, and peers using a variety of digital-age media and formats

**d.** model and facilitate effective use of current and emerging digital tools to locate, analyze, evaluate, and use information resources to support research and learning

## 4. Promote and Model Digital Citizenship and Responsibility

Teachers understand local and global societal issues and responsibilities in an evolving digital culture and exhibit legal and ethical behavior in their professional practices. Teachers:

**a.** advocate, model, and teach safe, legal, and ethical use of digital information and technology, including respect for copyright, intellectual property, and the appropriate documentation of sources

**b.** address the diverse needs of all learners by using learner-centered strategies and providing equitable access to appropriate digital tools and resources

**c.** promote and model digital etiquette and responsible social interactions related to the use of technology and information

**d.** develop and model cultural understanding and global awareness by engaging with colleagues and students of other cultures using digital-age communication and collaboration tools

## 5. Engage in Professional Growth and Leadership

Teachers continuously improve their professional practice, model lifelong learning, and exhibit leadership in their school and professional community by promoting and demonstrating the effective use of digital tools and resources. Teachers:

a.  participate in local and global learning communities to explore creative applications of technology to improve student learning

b.  exhibit leadership by demonstrating a vision of technology infusion, participating in shared decision making and community building, and developing the leadership and technology skills of others

c.  evaluate and reflect on current research and professional practice on a regular basis to make effective use of existing and emerging digital tools and resources in support of student learning

d.  contribute to the effectiveness, vitality, and self-renewal of the teaching profession and of their school and community

*© 2008 International Society for Technology in Education (ISTE), www.iste.org. All rights reserved.*

# CD Contents

Unit Activities, Handouts, and Rubrics

## Unit 1 ▪ Le Moyen Âge en France
*CoBaLTT Project (Content-Based Language Teaching with Technology)*

Unit 1 Activities Descriptions

Unit 1 Activity 1,  Handout 1—Introduction au Moyen Âge en France

Handout 2—Introduction au Moyen Âge en France

Handout 3—Introduction au Moyen Âge en France

Unit 1 Activity 2,  Handout 1—Des conflits et des fléaux au Moyen Âge

Handout 2—Des conflits et des fléaux au Moyen Âge

Unit 1 Activity 3,  Handout 1—La féodalité

Handout 2—La féodalité

Unit 1 Activity 4,  Handout 1—Des créations artistiques au Moyen Âge

Handout 2—Des créations artistiques au Moyen Âge

Handout 3—Des créations artistiques au Moyen Âge

Unit 1 Activity 5,  Handout 1—La vie de Charlemagne

Handout 2—La vie de Charlemagne

Handout 3—La vie de Charlemagne

Unit 1 Activity 6,  Handout 1—Assessment

Handout 2—Assessment

Handout 3—Assessment

Handout 4—Assessment

Unit 1 Rubrics from Appendix A for Le Moyen Âge en France

- Rubric for Oral Presentation

- Rubric for Written Version of Presentation

- Rubric for Assessment of NETS•S—Technology Use for Final Project

- Rubric for Skit (from Activity 4)

## Unit 2 ▪ Les Stéréotypes des Français
*CoBaLTT Project (Content-Based Language Teaching with Technology)*

Unit 2 Activities Descriptions

Unit 2 Activity 1, Handout 1— Stereotype Simulation
Self-Assessment Checklist for Web Browsing

Handout 2— Stereotype Simulation
Brainstorming

Handout 3— Stereotype Simulation
Guide d'analyse des stéréotypes

Unit 2 Activity 2, Handout 1— Stereotypes of Americans
Guide d'analyse des stéréotypes

Unit 2 Activity 3, Handout 1— America Views France
Présentations

Unit 2 Activity 4, Handout 1— Truth and Stereotypes
La vérité et les stéréotypes

Handout 2— Truth and Stereotypes
Les articles et les stéréotypes

Unit 2 Activity 5, Handout 1— Assessment
Directions for the Final Project

Handout 2— Assessment
Rubric for the Final Project (student-oriented version)

Unit 2 Rubrics from Appendix A for Les Stéréotypes des Français

- Rubric for NETS•S Assessment—Multimedia Presentation Project
- Rubric for Final Project

## Unit 3 ▪ Carole Fredericks: Music Is Only the Beginning
*Iowa State: The National K–12 Foreign Language Resource Center*

Unit 3 Activities Descriptions

Unit 3 Activity 1, Handout 1— Researching Carole Fredericks
Research Questions

Unit 3 Activity 2, Handout 1— Interpreting "Un, deux, trois"
Cloze Exercise

Handout 2— Interpreting "Un, deux, trois"
Song Lyrics

Unit 3 Activity 3, Handout 1— Interpreting the Music Video for "Un, deux, trois"
Questions on Lyrics for "Un, deux, trois"

Unit 3 Activity 4, Handout 1— Creating the Presentation (student-oriented rubrics)
Group Presentation Rubrics—Rubric for Assesssment
of Oral Presentation, Rubric for Assessment of National
Foreign Language Standards, and Rubric for Assessment
of NETS·S

Unit 3 Rubrics from Appendix A for Carole Fredericks: Music Is Only the Beginning

- Rubric for Oral Presentation

- Rubric for Assessment of NETS·S

- Rubric for Assessment of National Foreign Language Standards

## Unit 4 ▪ The Culture and Literature of Francophone West Africa
*Iowa State: The National K–12 Foreign Language Resource Center*

Unit 4 Activities Outline for CD

Unit 4 Activity 1 Geography of Francophone West Africa
Descriptions and Handouts: 1a, 1b, 2a, 2b

Unit 4 Activity 2 Country Profiles: Côte d'Ivoire and Sénégal
Descriptions and Handouts: 1, 2

Unit 4 Activity 3 CFA Francs
Descriptions and Handouts: 1, 2, 3, 4, and Key

Unit 4 Activity 4 Money and Culture
Descriptions and Handouts: 1, 2

Unit 4 Activity 5 African Oral Tradition
Descriptions and Handouts: 1, 2, 3

Unit 4 Activity 6 La Légende baoulé
Descriptions and Handouts: 1, 2a, 2b, 3, and Key

Unit 4 Activity 7 Structure Practice in Folktales
Descriptions and Handouts: 1, 2, and Key

Unit 4 Activity 8 (Le Pagne noir) and 9 (Cendrillon): Comparison of Folktales
Descriptions and Handouts: 1a, 1b, 1c, 2, and Key

Unit 4 Activity 8 Story: Le Pagne noir

Unit 4 Activity 9 Story: Cendrillon

CD Contents

Unit 4 Activity 10  Conte Original (Original Folktale)
Descriptions and Handout 1

Unit 4 Rubrics from Appendix A for Culture and Literature of Francophone West Africa

- Rubric for Oral Presentation

- Rubric for Assessment of NETS•S

- Rubric for Assessment of National Foreign Language Standards

If you like
# Technology-Infused French
you'll also like these related titles from ISTE.

## Global Education
### Using Technology to Bring the World to Your Students

By Laurence Peters

"An essential companion for teachers…who want to…foster a deeper understanding of what it means to live and learn in an interconnected world."

— Margaret Honey, President and CEO, New York Hall of Science

Discover how students can connect with their peers across geographical boundaries, expand their knowledge of the world, and increase their interest in what they are learning. Through advances in internet technology, including web 2.0 tools, any classroom can connect globally. Get started with *Global Education*.

**ISTE Member Price $22.37**
Nonmember Price $31.95

## Videoconferencing for K–12 Classrooms
### A Program Development Guide, Second Edition

By Camille Cole, Kecia Ray, and Jan Zanetis

Videoconferencing offers the potential to link classrooms worldwide and exposes students to places and people who simply can't be reached otherwise. This book includes a comprehensive review of current (and near-future) options for building an effective videoconferencing program, helping you make your classroom truly global.

**ISTE Member Price $26.57**
Nonmember Price $37.95

Visit the ISTE Bookstore, **iste.org/bookstore**, or browse the catalog, **iste.org/catalog** ⟩ iste.

If you like
# Technology-Infused French
you'll also like these related titles from ISTE.

## Web 2.0
### New Tools, New Schools

By Gwen Solomon and Lynne Schrum

"A good read for those without any knowledge of Web 2.0 as well as experienced users."

—*District Administration*

*Web 2.0: New Tools, New Schools* provides a comprehensive overview of the emerging web 2.0 technologies and their use in the classroom and in professional development. Topics include blogging as a natural tool for writing instruction, wikis and their role in project collaboration, and podcasting as a useful means of presenting information and ideas.

**ISTE Member Price $24.47**
Nonmember Price $34.95

## Web 2.0
### How-To for Educators

By Gwen Solomon and Lynne Schrum

"*Web 2.0 How-To for Educators*…should be at the hands of every technology-minded teacher."

—*Midwest Book Review*

"Can't recommend it highly enough…five stars out of five."

—*Tech & Learning*

In this companion book, the authors of the best-selling *Web 2.0: New Tools, New Schools* introduce you to more web 2.0 tools. Using a simple formula for each concept, the book describes *what* the tool is, *when* you should use it, *why* it is useful, *who* is using it, *how* you can use the tool, and *where* you can find additional resources.

**ISTE Member Price $24.47**
Nonmember Price $34.95

Visit the ISTE Bookstore, **iste.org/bookstore**, or browse the catalog, **iste.org/catalog**   iste.